WITHDRAWN

Robinson Jeffers:
Fragments of an Older Fury
By Brother Antoninus

Oyez : 1968

Contents

Foreword

Not Without Wisdom   1

The Giant Hand   9

Post Mortem   21

The Beauty of God   57

Hellenistics   67

The Far Cast Spear   99

The Poet is Dead   163

List of Works Cited

Index of Names

Acknowledgements

The author and publisher express their thanks to those who have granted permission to reprint previously published or copyright material.

From *In Defense of Reason* by Yvor Winters. Alan Swallow, Publisher. Copyright 1937, 1947 by Yvor Winters. Pages 33-34. Reprinted by permission of the executors of the Alan Swallow Estate.

From *The Hero with a Thousand Faces* by Joseph Campbell. Bollingen Series XVII. Copyright 1949 by Bollingen Foundation, New York. Distributed by Pantheon Books. Pages 25-26, 30-31, 33, 34, 35, 51, 58, 36-37, 388, 193, 216;

from *The Collected Works of C.G. Jung*, translated by R.F.C. Hull. Volume 7, *Two Essays on Analytical Psychology*. Bollingen Series XX.7. 2nd edition, copyright 1966 by Bollingen Foundation, New York. Distributed by Pantheon Books. Pages 233-234;

from *Archetypal Images in Greek Religion* by C. Kerenyi, translated from the German by Ralph Manheim. Volume 1, *Prometheus*. Bollingen Series LXV.1. Copyright 1963 by Bollingen Foundation, New York. Distributed by Pantheon Books. Page 3; and

from *The King and the Corpse* by Heinrich Zimmer, completed and edited by Joseph Campbell. Bollingen Series XI. 2nd edition, copyright 1956 by Bollingen Foundation, New York. Distributed by Pantheon Books. Page 310, notes 1 and 2; reprinted by permission of Bollingen Foundation.

From *Shine, Perishing Republic* by Rudolph Gilbert. Copyright 1936 by Bruce Humphries, Inc. Pages 109-110.

From *The Everlasting Man* by G.K. Chesterton. Dodd, Mead & Company, publishers. Page 58.

From "Robinson Jeffers and the Torches of Violence" by Frederic I. Carpenter, in *The Twenties: Poetry and Prose*, edited by Richard E. Langford & William E. Taylor. Copyright © 1966 by Everett/Edwards, inc., Deland, Florida, publishers. Page 15. Reprinted by permission of the publishers.

From *The White Goddess* by Robert Graves. Amended and enlarged edition, Vintage Books, 1958. Copyright 1948 by Robert Graves. Page 12. Reprinted by permission of Farrar, Straus & Giroux, Inc., publishers.

vii

ix

From *Robinson Jeffers* by Mercedes Cunningham Monjian. © 1958, University of Pittsburgh Press. Pages 84, 83. Reprinted by permission of the University of Pittsburgh Press.

From *The Portable Nietszche*, translated by Walter Kaufmann. Copyright 1954 by The Viking Press, Inc.

From *Robinson Jeffers* by William Van Wyck. Ward Ritchie Press. Reprinted by permission of the publisher.

For permission to print unpublished lines from the galley proofs of *The Women at Point Sur* in the Robinson Jeffers Collection, Yale Collection of American Literature, thanks are given to Donnan Jeffers and to Donald Gallup, Curator of the Collection of American Literature, Yale University Liberary.

Fragments of an Older Fury

foreword

With the publication of this book it will be five years since the death of Robinson Jeffers, and already the pendulum of critical regard is swinging back in his favor. The appearance of the posthumous volume *The Beginning and the End* evoked reviews that were generally friendly, and even the quarterlies, traditionally the last holdouts against so-called "anti-intellectualists," began to take a fresh look. Joseph Bennett wrote in *The Hudson Review:*

> The qualities that Aiken lacks, Jeffers has; perhaps too much so: he is irresistibly and unstably poetic. The furious impetus, the flux of sexual passion, the panther-like leap: harsh nature with the limp rabbit bleeding in her claws. Yet it's good, dramatic, exciting; it does not lull us like Aiken's staid and worthy buzz. This volume, his last, *The Beginning and the End*, contains some of the best work Jeffers has produced. I would say, on the basis of it, that Jeffers' reputation might be in for a renaissance.

The publication of his shorter poems in paperback, so long delayed, also indicates a rekindling of public attention, and new anthologies continue to feature his work. As I write, his collected letters are being prepared for publication, and a biography has been announced.

These facts make less urgent the task which this book set out to do: originally my ambition was nothing less than to effect a major reconsideration of the achievement of Jeffers as an American poet. The attempt was valid, certainly, but alas it must be held responsible in good measure for the defensive tone, the expostulatory urgency of much that I have uttered. Actually, Jeffers' old antagonists are themselves dying off, and a new generation appears ready to look at him with eyes unbiased by the bitter literary wars of the thirties and forties. Even old hostilities mellow. When I spoke recently to an elderly critic, now retired from academic life but still productive, and gently admonished him for his dismissal of my master, he smiled ruefully and replied, "Did I? When you are young you have battles to fight, and I fought mine. But I confess I can no longer read my early criticism. It is too painful to me now."

The first of these essays was written as a simple tribute to Robinson Jeffers at the time of his death and was published in *The Critic*. In it I sought principally to define my own relationship to him rather than institute the general revaluation, though something of that did creep in. But the main concern was tribute not defense, and it is therefore more personal than the rest of the book — save, of course, the elegy at the close. Both these pieces, by virtue of this elegiac temper, do stand somewhat apart from the main direction of the work, and I hope this concern, this note of personal implication and gravity, is not out of character in a work as polemical as parts of this one do become.

The next two pieces were actually written earlier, my first tentative attempts to reconstitute the Jeffersian image. They were, however, never published. "Post Mortem," despite appearances to the contrary, was written first — in the late fifties, I think — and "The Giant Hand" followed at the beginning of the present decade. Perhaps the fact that Jeffers was still alive prevented me from pressing more energetically for immediate publication. Chronologically, the closing piece, "The Poet is Dead," really belongs, as I have said, with the opening tribute, for the period and the mood are much the same. It was published first in *Ramparts* of Christmas 1963, where my review of *The Beginning and the End* also appeared. This review does take up again the work of revaluation, is avowedly polemical, and continues the development of my attempt beyond that established by "Post Mortem" and "The Giant Hand." Following the *Ramparts* appearance the Auerhahn Press of San Francisco issued *The Poet is Dead* in a limited edition of two hundred copies, with my note on its contribution to the San Francisco Poetry Festival. This note is here reprinted with the elegy, sustaining the same personal element that set apart the "Tribute" and the elegy itself.

It was at this point that the editors of Oyez approached me with an eye to presenting in book form my pieces on Jeffers. As I assembled them it became apparent that certain large areas of relevance in regard to the poet remained unexplored, and that if I were to offer the public anything so ambitious as a complete book these matters ought to be touched on. One such topic was that of Jeffers' so-called fascism. Travelling about the country on reading junkets I was surprised to find on campuses this lingering impression from the thirties, and I determined to engage the issue, and discover why the matter was so far less serious to me than it apparently was among them. Another matter was the problem of *The Women at Point Sur*, which Jeffers considered his key work. It was too vast to attempt a thorough-going exposition for the proposed volume, but I thought an introduction to such a study might touch on some of the difficulties long associated with this complex poem.

Here, then, are seven essays and an elegy. They constitute all I can presently articulate about my old master, a man whom I knew deeply in spirit but never in life, one who was too near to me, too dear to me, too terrifying to me, and too necessary for me, back at that finding of the self which makes the pivot of a life, ever to face in this flesh.

Brother Antoninus
May 25, 1966
Kentfield, California

1

Not Without Wisdom

Written on the occasion of the poet's death, and printed, together with a poem by Tim Reynolds, in *The Critic*, June-July, 1962, under the title "A Tribute to Robinson Jeffers." Primarily a memorial, this paper also seeks to define the author's relationship to Jeffers as a disciple.

> *Jeffers has re-established the position of the poet as one of singular dignity and courage. He is neither voiceless nor without his readers; and he is not without wisdom in seeming to await the verdict of posterity.*
>
> —HORACE GREGORY
> *Poet Without Critics*

R obinson Jeffers died on January 19, at home in Tor House, Carmel, having just turned seventy-five. With the passing of every substantial literary figure it is customary to say that his death marks "the end of an epoch." This is not true of Jeffers in the way it was true of Joyce and Yeats, and will be true of Eliot and Pound. But it is true, I think, in the way it will be of Frost. Neither of them coterie poets, each hewed out a kind of epochal place for himself in the literature of his time. Among contemporary poets, European or American, Jeffers is unique in that he has been the only one to project and sustain a truly cosmic vision of man, induct a whole cosmology, as Homer and Dante and Milton did before him. I am speaking here in terms of conception, what is called vision, rather than presuming to anticipate the judgment of history as to the æsthetic achievement. Though I myself do not doubt that achievement, and suspect that the "excesses" of his earlier enthusiasts are very near the truth, his latter-day friends have mostly learned to be more cautious. His deniers, as is well known, regard such comparisons as preposterous.

Radcliffe Squires, in his book *The Loyalties of Robinson Jeffers*, holds that one reason Jeffers never attained a prestige consonant with his stature is that he has lacked disciples, and goes on to say he clearly desired none. As far as I know I am the only disciple Jeffers ever had, and it is a fact that I lived within a hundred miles of him all my life (save for the war years) and never met him. To be the only disciple of a major poet, especially one who detests them, is as disconcerting for the disciple as it is for the master; the embarrassment is mutual.

3

He had his advocates, certainly, but true disciples are more than believers; they are in some ways extensions of the master's own self. Thus I was not a follower in the European sense of one who furthers an artist's cause, or even in the sense of one who studies a craft at a master's feet. With me it was something more like the Oriental relationship of the sybarite to the *guru*. As Koestler describes it in *The Lotus and the Robot*, "It is not his words that matter, but his presence — they breathe him, they imbibe him, it is a process of acquiring merit by spiritual osmosis." That is the way I took to Jeffers. Out of his books I soaked him up, and it was only secondarily his ideas or even his technique that absorbed me. What I sought was a presence, a spiritual and a psychological substance. The force from his pages hit me as something almost physical .

I had been trying unsuccessfully to write poetry for almost five years when I discovered the work of Jeffers. This was back in 1934. As a Californian I had no traditional culture to support me the way a New Englander or a Southerner has. The nineteenth-century models given me in high school and college I found respectable but baffling, because they could in no way engage my actual need. As for transcendental values, my own father's agnosticism had left me virtually starved, almost desperate. When I encountered Jeffers it was essentially a religious conversion, my first one. Not only so, it was the intellectual awakening. For the first time I grasped the corruptness of man and the reality of an Absolute against which that corruptness must be measured. For the first time I knew there is a God, and I knew where I was going to find Him — before my very eyes, as He is bodied forth in prime Nature. And I knew that place no longer had to be the Lake Country, or Nantucket, or fish-shaped Paumonak, or the Mississippi. The place was California, the Coast. I saw that He was intensely, incredibly alive in my own region.

Nor was this all. In the terrible narratives, in the themes of incest and patricide, violence and destruction, I found the outlet for all the unconscious passion I had not realized was obsessing me. We were both sons of fathers twenty years older than the women they married. Upon us the mother projected that fateful fascination youthful maternity so often bestows upon the first male to open the womb. Heirs of blind Oedipus (Squires' view that because Jeffers thought kindly of his father he did not suffer from the oedipal flaw I find astonishing), we transposed the maternal *imago* to unspoliated nature, and projected the deep paternal hostility upon civilization and its structures. Out of this blockage he wrote the narratives and I drank them in, though when I myself came to write, certain qualifying differences emerged. His father was a man of the mind, a minister and a scholar. Mine was a wandering immigrant Norwegian musician and printer. Whereas his work is centered upon the exposition of ideas, my own moves toward subjective states of being, tonal values, and the shape of the poem on the page. In the beginning these differences were not apparent to me; I simply breathed his air. And if, in the living of my life, I went a different way from his, it was because, I suppose, I realized that there was no use doing over what he had done before me. One may, for a time, imitate an art; to imitate a life is fatal. I had not, furthermore, the income to secure my isolation. More crucially, he met the woman who would cultivate and condition the primordial attitude, focus the underlying tension in his nature. With me, Providence decreed a different eventuality. I met a Catholic.

Given the archetype, we each needed an idiom commensurate with the disruptive energies that troubled us. Where he found it I am not prepared to say; the matter is disputed. I found it in him. The stricter verse forms my teachers had so earnestly sought to impress upon me passed over my mind like cloud shadows on the sea, leaving no trace. They were too tight, struc-

tured too closely upon the rational principle, too symbolic of
the culture I could not relate to, to accommodate the blindnesses
within me. But in Jeffers, in the loose shovelling rhythms, in the
long grappling lines, in the uncoiling constructions and the volcanic images, I found the perfect mode – perfect in the sense of
truth-to-source. Between the "heresy of expressive form" and
the "heresy of *a priori* correct form" lies the orthodoxy (orthodox because universal) of authentic approximation, truth to self,
original causal adequation. But reading Jeffers, the indoctrination took so thoroughly I was another five years working my
way out of it, finding my own voice. That I did at last find it
I have no doubt, for when my early volumes were synthesized
and published by New Directions in 1948, with all that perva-
sive Jeffersian influence carefully screened out by my editor,
and my secondary Lawrencian element coaxed into prominence
by the blurb, whatever the critics scored me for (and given my
credentials they looked for everything), they did not score me
for Jeffers. Not one of them noticed my birth certificate.

Is it not ironic that a man the stature of Jeffers should be prevented the attestation of any influence at all, even in the only
place it could possibly exist, in the work of his one disciple? It
is as if fate, in the effort to deny him any place, left no stone
unturned. But after all, given my subsequent reversal, given my
ultimate allegiance, he would, were he aware of it, have thanked
his stars. A loyal disciple is only a clutter; if he is good there
emerges the problem of competition; if he is bad, there remains
the problem of apology. But if he is an apostate, both these
problems congeal in simple embarrassment. That a spiritual son
should have renounced pantheism for Rome would have dis-
gusted, but hardly surprised him. "How many children," he had
cried, "run to Mother Church, Father State!" When a couple of
years ago I at last sent him a book it was my Catholic poems. No
balm to him that I should inscribe it "to the greatest living poet." Reading that he must have spat upon the ground.

So he went almost unhonored among poets, and he cared not a damn. But I do. To me it is a disappointment that my second mentor, Kenneth Rexroth, to whom I am so profoundly indebted in other ways, should scorn my first one, who deserves better. Given Rexroth's origins as an experimentalist it is perhaps only to be expected that he should reject Jeffers. But that Kenneth could not see his way to centering his West Coast movement around the achievement of Jeffers consigns it, in my view, to insubstantiality and attenuation. Surely, if you are going to speak of "the disaffiliated," Jeffers is the granddaddy of them all. None of our lesser talents can fill the hiatus, the yawning gap left by his exclusion. And as for the "Pacific Basin Culture," any attempt to promote the Californian contribution to that without reference to Jeffers is to hoist the tent without the pole. But that is the way it was meant to be. It is the doom and the glory of Robinson Jeffers that he is destined to survive absolutely alone. You might say he *willed* it that way.

So now he is gone, an aged eagle that long outlived his mate, and had no wish to live. The decade of bitterness preceding his death is hardly surprising, given his attitude, given the temper of his mind, the tenor of his soul. The obsequies, could he have read them, would hardly have interested him. In substance all that had been uttered decades ago, and no one found anything very original to say. Perhaps the best thing written about him in recent years is the poem by Tim Reynolds published in *Poetry*. I can think of no better way to close this tribute than to ask that it be reprinted here. If he ever saw Tim's poem, I think he would have been pleased with it, pleased to recognize himself as its unacknowledged subject. As for me, I have placed his name in the roster of the departed, to be included in The Office of the Dead. That he no longer despises what in this life he did not understand I have no doubt, for his generosity of heart must have been marvelous. As it is, I can do nothing more for him now. But I have, as he once said in another context, "paid my birth-dues."

THE STONE-MASON
By Tim Reynolds

The stone-mason seeketh for work in all manner of hard stone.
When he hath finished it his arms are destroyed, and he is weary. . . .

Lying on sand where mountain streams break through, I have seen
at night, on bridges, streaks of black across the burning stars,
headlights; whose light, passing the concrete slats, quite suddenly
shut like a fan: driving the high cliff road, coming slowly around
a granite shoulder, I saw once a comber of white fog poised
so like a wave, so huge, so heavily, that I stopped the car, braced
for the fall: I have watched hawks in updraft effortlessly lifting,
wings wide: seen redwoods' strength and cypresses' warped
*   endurance;*
sea-carved granite headlands plumbing sheer down, bicep-curved,
*   to sea;*
half-seen deer; seen but never freshly, all this having been claimed by
him who staked out this land, these permanences, unalienably for his.

And I have seen him, who quarried out and worked this raw existence
the stone-mason: seen him walking by day in shade of the big trees
framing the tower of boulders he hung against the sky, back broad
and hard-handed — but bent, but slow, after a spent life of building
something more lucid than any visible light, lighter than fog,
lifting still higher than hawk-flight, yet comprehending most things
hard, pure and durable, something tough as backbones of coastal
*   hills*
and spacious, like a tower, with a solid place to stand on top —
watched him picking his way along rock shores at night, alone
under the stars he loves (which, weary now, burn steadily, if far,
fragments of an older fury).

2

The Giant Hand

Written in rebuttal of the critic Randall Jarrell
whose remarks on Jeffers were delivered in a principal
lecture at the National Poetry Festival sponsored
by the Library of Congress, Washington, D.C., in
the fall of 1962, and were printed as "Fifty
Years of American Poetry" in *The Prairie Schooner*,
Spring, 1963.

Four pelicans went over the house,
Sculled their worn oars over the courtyard:
I saw that ungainliness
Magnifies the idea of strength . . .
　　　　　　—Pelicans

O ne mark of the major poet," it has been written, "is his power to seize the reader with a giant hand and carry him out of himself, even before he grasps what is being said." Whatever reservations one might hold as to the achievement of Robinson Jeffers, I think few will deny that among American poets he possessed this power to an uncommon degree. Open the *Selected Poetry* almost anywhere, his first lines establish instantly the quality of his presence. Grave, somber, vibrant, compelling, elusive yet emphatic, remarkably concrete yet strangely mythical, each initiates unfailingly the substance of what is to follow: "The old voice of the ocean, the bird-chatter of little rivers"; "Point Joe has teeth and has torn ships"; "The clapping blackness of the wings of pointed cormorants"; "The days shorten, the south blows wide for showers now"; "I am heaping the bones of the old mother"; "Old garden of grayish and ochre lichen"; "Stone-cutters fighting time with marble"; — poem after poem, the opening phrases establish the immediate, unmistakable presence. Truly, the Giant Hand is beginning its work, reaching for the reader to carry him out of himself, even before he grasps what is being said.

It is the unconscious signature of all great expression, and it covers a multitude of sins. Virginia Woolf acknowledged this when she wrote: "The success of the masterpieces seems to lie not so much in their freedom from faults — indeed we tolerate the grossest errors in them all—but in the immense persuasiveness of a mind which has completely mastered its perspective." Provided he is blessed with genius the faults of a writer are, then, if not irrelevant, certainly powerless to hurt him — the formula allows him, grandly, the *grossest* errors. What covers these lapses is something incalculable yet utterly redemptive: *the immense persuasiveness of a mind which has completely mastered its perspective.* We have been seized by that Giant Hand, and are carried out of ourself. For the time being, we exist in another world.

But the history of letters shows that the initial impact of genius, like that of grace, is instinctively resisted. The Giant Hand may be in play, and we may sense it, but we possess more than one recourse to evade the consequence of its directives. That "immense persuasiveness," the need and effort to convince, is the chief sign of a point of view markedly contrary to the attitude of the time. If this were not so, there would be no necessity for the plea. A few decades or a few centuries later, men commonly recognize the presence of genius, because it no longer costs anything to do so; the issues that gave it birth are sufficiently resolved with the passage of time, and experiencing the compelling presence in all its potentiality, men wonder how we, his contemporaries, could have been so blind. We could tell them. In the case of Jeffers, what he preaches, and preaches trenchantly, is utterly unacceptable not only to our prevailing temper, but more especially to our desperate hopes, and all the presence of power will not compel us to jeopardize the future we desire by celebrating a work that repudiates it utterly. Rather we have a critical formula at hand to meet the situation: concede the power but condemn the matter; discount the presence and denounce the faults. Having made such a bed, let the man lie in it. Let him take his chances with the future.

And so he will. And after his hostile century, spent, has left him, immured like some prehistoric animal in the glacier of history, men's fascination with their origins will lead them back, and under that interest his larger relevance will, I am convinced, emerge. Exhumed, the awesome presence will be recognized, for it is unmistakable, as unmistakable as that potentiality we sense in the configuration of those beasts of the past our museums reveal to us—the rough angularities, the direct operative disposition of bone, sinew, and hide, the ferocious outmoded armaments of tusk and claw, and especially that ineluctable lonely aspect of a creature made for permanence inhospitably born into an era of change — all these will be recognized and admired. As an Ancestor, Jeffers' primitivism, so reprehensible today, will become, in the urbanized decadence ahead, the man's greatest attractiveness; and the proud aloofness, so affronting to our gregariousness, will distinguish him from the more transient accomplishments of our favorites, transmuted by the resolving increase of distance into an engaging singularity. Then the Giant Hand will be felt in truth, the immemorial presence will be valorized by exclamations of wonder and awe, and, at long last, another Great Poet will be received into the canon of our literature.

Or so I believe. And hence, one can accept the stubborn disparagement, whenever some requirement breaks the silence critical disaffection has cast about him, and compels his consideration. One can accept it because one knows it must be, but one cannot concur in it. In an address of special significance because it was made before the first National Poetry Festival at the Library of Congress, the critic Randall Jarrell took up the case of Jeffers by making the customary acknowledgement of the poet's residual assets: "Robinson Jeffers has taken an interesting and unusual part of the world and has described it, narrated some overpowering events that have occurred in it, with great — but crude and approximate — power." This severely qualified attribution completes the sanction; the rest is stricture:

> He celebrates the survival of the fittest, the war of all against all, but his heart goes out to animals rather than to human beings, to minerals rather than to animals, since he despises the bonds and qualifications of existence. Because of all this his poems do not have

the exactness and concision of the best poetry; his style and temperament, his whole world-view, are to a surprising extent a matter of simple exaggeration. The motto of his work is "More! more!" — but as Tolstoy says, "A wee bit omitted, overemphasized, or exaggerated in poetry, and there is no contagion"; and Frost, bearing him out, says magnificently: "A very little of anything goes a long way in a work of art."

The force of these statements lies, of course, not so much in their originality as in their orthodoxy and the occasion of their utterance, for they are unquestionably the received opinion among American critics today; nevertheless they are seated upon an over-simplification. For since the actual "states of being" the poet celebrates are registered with undeniable power, it follows that if that power is "crude and approximate" then crudity and approximation must reside in the states of being themselves. They are not failures of taste or defects of awareness, or else they could not be called powerful, for power in literature can only emerge from power in life. That crudity and that approximation must constitute the actuality of the matter under registration — a factor which brings the Tolstoy quote decisively into perspective. The estimate of excess, whether it be by omission, or over-emphasis or exaggeration, cannot, in art, be measured by *a priori* criteria — the immemorial error of critics — but devolves by reference to the subject matter itself. And this not by recourse to the discredited theory that the chaos of the world can only be rendered in a chaotic style, but by virtue of the principle that the initiating locus of energy (the archetype) must determine the configuration of its effect. To maintain otherwise is to betray the fact that the actual motive in play is not to register the naked truth of the subject, its essence, its truth of being, but is rather to situate it in our mental world, a secondary thing, locate it in some power-complex in the ego (Tradition, Politics, Religion, etc.), imposing definition from without. While all art is admittedly born of the tension between these two psychological polarities, the *creative* writer invariably takes the plunge into the depths of the former. Nietzsche has said: "Regarding artists of all kinds, I now avail myself of this main distinction: is it the *hatred* against life or the *excess* of life which has here become creative? In Goethe, for example, the excess became creative; in Flaubert, hatred." The language is extreme. But it is customary to charge Jeffers with hatred of life, while as a matter of fact he stands with the great exemplars of excess. In an age that has canonized Flaubert is it any wonder that he is unforgiven?

Never pretending to approximate in verse the conscience or the discipline of the urbanized intellectual, a task he willingly renounces as the rightful province of others, Jeffers has rather chosen to resuscitate the opposite: that maimed and blinded forebear in ourself, whose heart "goes out to animals rather than to human beings, to minerals rather than to animals," because, crippled by our excruciating excess of ratiocination, it has been allowed no place in our sanitary world. What the poet despises, therefore, are not the authentic bonds and qualifications of existence, but their cerebricized substitutes as found in our culture and our intellectuals. How can such a task be discounted by a literary mentality trained to value the tremendous uses of the probe toward naked evil itself in the fascinations of a Baudelaire or a Rimbaud? There is something almost maddening about the opacity of intelligent men in the presence of a manifest but uncongenial greatness. Something fearful and redemptive in themselves, more awesome than any of the bonds and qualifications by which they live, is being prodded from its long sleep, and they abandon it, not in fear so much as in disdain, to a terrible stillbirth.

The point is, then, that while Jeffers' interest is indeed in the extremes of sensation, he registers this extremity with telling accuracy and in fact with powerful concision. But in so doing he is never content to rest in even these extremes as terminals, induced "for their own sake," as some have accused. Rather, pushing beyond them with an over-reaching thirst, he shoulders inexorably toward an ultimate reality. This thirst for otherness through the extremes of sensation, this capacity to rise out of torment and seize right and left ingesting toward totality, incites Jarrell to taunt "More! more!" and offer the foil of Frost's New England succinctness. But Wallace Stevens can write in contradiction and with equal authority: "One of the consequences of the ordination of style is not to limit it, but to enlarge it, not to impoverish it, but to enrich and liberate it." When a poem fails to survive it is probable that it suffers from a deficiency, not from an excess — a deficiency of prime energy, usually, that has led the poet to settle for a term too far short of an ultimate to have anything but a contemporary interest, or a scruple of applicative zeal that pruned too severely the natural luxuriance of the vine: Nietzsche's "hatred against life." Certain critical mentalities, like certain scientific ones, take energy for granted, and value only the processes of reduction and refinement, a sin of pride. But actually it is the tolerance and indeed the relishing of a surplus of energy, energy in uncheckable abundance, that constitutes the prime ingredient of that mysterious syndrome, the awesome authority of the Giant Hand.

Yes, a little reflection goes a long way to show that the matter of degree, which is the issue here, rests within the nature of the material and its field of situation. A poet dealing with epic material is dealing with the excesses of life, which are not the invention of romantics, though romantics have luxuriated in them, but are hearted in reality itself, a matter which has long been known. Scripture declares:

> The horseleach hath two daughters, crying, "Give, give."
> There are three things that are never satisfied,

Yea, four that say not, "Enough":
The grave; and the barren womb;
The earth that is not satisfied with water;
And the fire that saith not, "Enough."

To these archetypes the prophet might have added the imagination of the poet, for once it is fully in act it accepts no limit.
Even as an old man Jeffers shook in the excess of that insatiable
energy:

Peace in our time was never one of God's promises; but back and
   forth, die and live, burn and be damned,
The great heart beating, pumping into our arteries His terrible life.

By no means his finest passage, nevertheless the precise registration of this state of consuming and restless energy, of uncontainable urgency and intolerable unrest, is superb. Its very
looseness of texture (one of the chief means by which Jeffers
appropriates into consciousness the undifferentiated areas of
psychic awareness), its folding and unfolding extensions and
withdrawals, utterly befits it. And consider that *burn and be
damned*!—a fierce unchokable cry erupting within the engross-
ing slacked-tenseness of the shifting emotional fabric, to turn
the passage. It possesses the movement and energy of life; we
recognize again the unmistakable signature, for this mind has
completely mastered its perspective. The reach for otherness has
taken us into areas where the great transhuman values abide,
and we live, not our own life, but His. In this situation, out of
this material, we understand the horseleach; and the cry "More!
more!", unstanchable, is manifest in its truth. Caught there,
however momentarily, in the willing suspension of our disbelief, we cannot but assent.

*

It is not so. An editor, who is also a friend, returned this
paper with the comment, "I feel that you somehow don't make

your case convincing (not enough minute particulars, or something), and I think the reason is that you are so convinced yourself that you feel that the reader is too, right in the beginning." Well, it is true that I am convinced, or I shouldn't be writing the paper. Actually, my aim was to make that conviction palpable, tangible, and do this by taking the point of my awareness down somewhere near the source of my feeling about the *presence* of the man. I forgot that ours is a scientific age, and by virtue of the reflex of scientific values upon æsthetic ones, has developed into what Mr. Jarrell has himself, in conscious rebuke, dubbed the "Age of Criticism."

Given such an age the only emphasis the literate man feels he can permit himself, the only believable values he owns to, are those that are capable of the most severe qualifications. Thus an acutely analytical treatise finds print immediately, and we, provided a certain aloofness of tone reassures us that we are in the presence of a detached mentality, ride along on what are actually the most sweeping generalizations — as we saw in Mr. Jarrell's swift-stroke dismissal of our poet. For in dismissal we are not asked to affirm anything. Like Romans at the gladiatorial contest, obsessed with mortality, we lean forward to see a man destroyed, and sigh only before the dispatch with which it is done. But if one seeks to affirm, to celebrate, to marvel in the work of any but the approved, then one must support his case with the most minute particulars, fabricate a tissue of inter-supporting details and cross-references, and, in the end, present to the world something as cold in its affirmation as the very temper of our dubiety itself, something as resistant, hard-faceted and achieved as what we like to call, pridefully, "the hard core of our thought."

Perhaps you demur. Perhaps, sensing my touchiness, you admonish me gently, hoping to be convinced: "Could you not, at least, give us *something*? Could you not, just for the moment, *demonstrate* what you affirm?" Certainly. But if I analyzed before your eyes the syllabic efficacy and powerful energy cross-laced and evocative in such an opening line as

> *Stone-cutters fighting time with marble, you foredefeated*
> *Challengers of oblivion . . .*

demonstrating how it immediately grasps the imagination with that Giant Hand, laying bare, in the abrupt juxtaposition of fighting *time* to cutting *stone*, striking the resonances of contained tonalities, grave, powerful, so marvellously compelling and yet so superbly relaxed, would you actually find it more "convincing"? I doubt it. Why? Because of what I have already said:"All the presence of power will not compel us to jeopardize the future we desire by acknowledging a work that repudiates it utterly."

Jeffers' career was like a Jeffers poem. It burst with shuddering impact upon the consciousness of his time. Men responded to his voice because he seemed to offer them deliverance from universal hysteria, the insane paradox of the Age of Jazz and the Age of Prohibition. Fascinated, they could not but listen; but, listening, they could hardly believe. It is the immemorial witness of the prophet, who must fascinate, compel, and then indict. Unfortunately, it is the indictment that is remembered, the fascination that is denied. With *Tamar* and with *Roan Stallion* men sprang up in acclaim, glimpsing a kind of violational freedom from the preoccupations that enveloped them, sensing the liberation that lies beyond the threshold of defiance, the cement walls of conformism. But with *Point Sur* they realized *what he was talking about*, and they were appalled. Now, only the counter-detachment of time will soften the aloof disapproval of the critical mind set on its established course of dissidence. This being so, nothing moves forward. In travelling about the country I am not hard put to find men who privately acknowledge the achievement of Jeffers. But publicly, that is to say, *in print*, we allow our enthusiasm only for that handful of certified authors who are the touchstones of contemporary cultural attitudes. To speak up for a maverick is not to be understood. But actually to *celebrate* where we are not understood is to jeopardize the respect of many colleagues, perhaps forfeit our own hard-won place in their esteem. And so, being human, we say nothing, and get on with our work.

Now I too must get on with mine, for a poet's office is his own compelling vision, the coaxing of the Muse. But she will not disapprove if I pause now and then to celebrate the memory of a noble man and a great artist. Nor will she object, I feel sure, if I take up cudgels to defend that greatness against men who reveal in everything they say how much they know of the literature of the past, the anguish and the ordeal of its makers, but who, in what they fail to say, reveal how little they have learned from it.

3 Post Mortem:
The Uses of Imprecision

Written as a venture in close analysis in
disproof of the supposition that the poetry of Jeffers
has little to yield to scrutiny in depth.

> *The poet, who wishes not to play games with words,*
> *His affair being to awake dangerous images*
> *And call the hawks . . .*
> *—Triad*

In the foregoing paper I raised the question of whether or not the minute analysis of a Jeffers poem could convince our time's prevalent dubiety that the man's undeniable power was centered in genuine artistry. I decided it would not. As is well known, close textual analysis is best performed upon a certain kind of densely fabricated work, poetry of the Metaphysical period, or, more recently, the neo-Metaphysical revival, and it is commonly admitted that some of the best modern poems do not fare very well when subjected to the rigors of *la explication de texte*. Nevertheless, despite this detriment, I have taken up one of Jeffers' powerful shorter poems and dissected it in the preferred fashion, line by line, and, where necessary, syllable by syllable, in the belief that, if the poem could be shown even to survive at the hands of a friendly critic, some of the onus of the frown of a hostile one might be redressed. In order properly to approach the poem itself, I shall begin with a few reflections on the role of the poet as it was originally determined for our time by one of our leading spokesmen and practitioners, Mr. Ezra Pound.

I

"It is the poet who protects the 'whole machinery of social and individual thought and order' against catastrophe through his heroic tribal role as purifier of the language." Mr. M. L. Rosenthal, in his *The Modern Poets*, recapitulates the testament of Pound, and demonstrates how he sought to accomplish this through "clarity, precision and vigor." Now these are classical values, certainly, and are indispensable to the well-being of culture. But while acknowledging their cruciality, it is necessary to point out that poets also attempt this task, this purification, in other ways, and chiefly through return to primordial sources. In doing so they lay aside the aforementioned objective values and adopt their opposites: the plunge back into archetypal approximation. What is being reclaimed is the subjective value of imprecision, of diffuseness, even, if necessary, of a kind of redolent ponderousness. Pound himself does this in his famous rendering of the Anglo-Saxon "Seafarer." As Rosenthal says, "Here Pound cultivates a heavy, lurching, even clumsy pounding of sound ... The effect is 'barbaric' and elemental, rhythmic as galley rowers are rhythmic; at the same time it underscores the rigors of seafaring life. While Pound actually stays very close to a literal translation of the text, he makes it a modern poem with archaic overtones."

> *Burgher knows not —*
> *He the prosperous man — what some perform*
> *Where wandering them widest draweth.*
> *So that but now my heart burst from my breastlock,*
> *My mood 'mid the mere-flood,*
> *Over the whale's acre, would wander wide.*
> *On earth's shelter cometh oft to me,*
> *Eager and ready, the crying lone-flyer,*
> *Whets for the whale-path the heart irresistibly,*
> *O'er tracks of ocean; seeing that anyhow*
> *My lord deems to me this dead life*
> *On loan and on land, I believe not*
> *That any earth-weal eternal standeth*
> *Save there be somewhat calamitous*
> *That, ere a man's tide go, turn it to twain.*
> *Disease or oldness or sword-hate*
> *Beats out the breath from doom-gripped body.*

This aspect of Pound's work was, of course, minimal. His decision to purify the language through clarity, precision, and vigor, emphatically threw the center of gravity toward objective norms of evaluation. The opposite attempt, so obvious in the practice of his great precursor Whitman, necessarily had to be attacked, despite his glance at the uses of archaism in "The Seafarer," because of its dangerously imprecise norms. He sensed that the future lay elsewhere.

With the outbreak of the Revolution of the Word before World War I, the two elements, purification through objective precision and purification through an imprecisionist return to archaic sources, found themselves allied against a decadent Establishment, but with the showy triumph of *vers libre* in the immediate postwar period, a victory culminating in the rout of the common enemy, the cleavage between the two points of view could only emerge with increasing decisiveness. Given the cultural disposition of the time, it was inevitable that although Whitman's massive source-seeking had actually begun the process of purification, Pound's precisionism, and his disciple Eliot's traditionalism, should in the end prevail as the two wings of the vanguard which would capture the period. The defeat of Whitman's norms can be glimpsed not only in the passing of the influence of Sandburg, Vachel Lindsay and John Gould Fletcher, but especially in the failure of such East Coast Jewish psalmists as James Oppenheim and Eli Siegel to extend Whitman's method; although their attempt, apparently lost through three decades, has been redeemed with great vigor in the work of their direct descendant, Allen Ginsberg, who launched the Beat Generation in the middle fifties.

At the time, however, two men, on the basis of certain adaptations and modifications, did succeed in surviving the Wave of the Future mounted by Pound and Eliot. The West Coast poet Robinson Jeffers and the Englishman D. H. Lawrence were each in his own way able to establish themselves upon the initial groundswell of general revolt. Then, in the Depression, the rise of doctrinaire proletarianism corrupted every aspect of literary culture it could infiltrate until, utterly discredited at last, it could only leave the field, after the war, to the triumph of a reactionary precisionist criticism and a highbrow poetry of impenetrable surfaces. Resisting either wing, Jeffers and Lawrence were both assailed, but each had the energy, the genius and the toughness of mind to persist despite the most extreme discouragement, and they leave behind them a body of work which has no peer in this *genre* except that of Whitman himself. That it was done by repudiation of everything the culture stood for, a price few were willing to pay, is true; but what has not been understood is that only such a repudiation enabled the recovery of verbal resources through a return to attitudes consonant with the roots of instinctual life. Laying aside the case of Lawrence in order to illustrate something of this recovery in the work of Jeffers, I should like to begin by recounting an incident.

II

One day in 1954, browsing in the monastery library, I picked up the book *Scotland of the Saints* by D. D. C. P. Mould. In her chapter "The Church in the North" she speaks of the penetration of Christianity into Ireland, and from one of the old poems she quotes the encounter between St. Patrick and the mythical Ossian, who confronts the saint with these words:

> *I once found shields and spears, dogs and beagles beneath thy walls;*
> *but today the Hill of the Feinne is under clerics and croziers.*
> *If the clans of Morna lived, your order would not be powerful; you*
> *would be put under restraint, you folk of the deceiving croziers.*
> *If Mac Lughdhach lived, and his six stalwart champions, your*
> *vestments would be torn before ever you should quit the Hill.*
> *If the Clan of Dubh-Dithreabh lived, if valient Caoilte lived, the din*
> *of bells and clerics would not be listened to in the Fort of Cruachan.*
> *If choice Raighne lived, and Caol Crodha son of Criomhthann, thy*
> *book would not long hold together, O man who readest*
> *from a bible.*
> *Thou man of the crooked staff, who hast made a presumptuous*

journey, thy staff would be in splinters if Osgar were on the spot.
If Mac Ui Dhuibhne lived, thou man of the crossed crozier, thy staff
  (and I should not be sorry) would be broken on a rock.
O man of the bell, if Diorraing were alive, I fancy he would soon
  shatter thy bell against the rock's face.
No wonder that I am mournful on this hill, O Patrick; I see not
  Mac Lughdhach, I see not the beloved throng.

I thought: Good Lord! Robinson Jeffers! And stepping down a few stacks I pulled out Untermeyer's *Anthology of American Poetry* seeking perhaps Jeffers' place-poem "Ossian's Grave," with its tremendous restorative "The mountains are alive; Tievebuilleagh lives, Trostan lives, Lurigethan lives;/And Aura, the black-faced sheep in the belled heather; and the swan-haunted loughs"; as if the primordial heroes that were dying in Ossian's day were once again awake and puissant.

I did not find "Ossian's Grave" in that collection, but what I came upon was just as germane to my purpose. It is the poem called "Post Mortem," a poem I had first read twenty years earlier. But scanning it there in the monastery walls, surrounded by so many centuries of accumulated Christian culture, having through years of monastic enclosure purged my mind of all the poem might have meant to me, Jeffers' utterance came into me with tremendous force. I thought: My God! How *pre-Christian* his mentality is! And I read it again, as a man turns an ancient stone in his hands, thumbing its texture to approximate out of the living surfaces something hidden within himself, shut from all his conscious orientation but ineluctably there, in his deeps, strangely called forth to life.

POST MORTEM

Happy people die whole, they are all dissolved in a moment, they
  have had what they wanted,
No hard gifts; the unhappy
Linger a space, but pain is a thing that is glad to be forgotten; but one

who has given
His heart to a cause or a country,
His ghost may spaniel it awhile, disconsolate to watch it. I was
*   wondering how long the spirit*
That sheds this verse will remain
When the nostrils are nipped, when the brain rots in its vault or
*   bubbles in the violence of fire*
To be ash in metal. I was thinking
Some stalks of the wood whose roots I married to the earth of this
*   place will stand five centuries;*
I held the roots in my hand,
The stems of the trees between two fingers: how many remote
*   generations of women*
Will drink joy from men's loins,
And dragged from between the thighs of what mothers will giggle at
*   my ghost when it curses the axemen,*
Gray impotent voice on the sea-wind,
When the last trunk falls? The women's abundance will have built
*   roofs over all this foreland;*
Will have buried the rock foundations
I laid here: the women's exuberance will canker and fail in its time
*   and like clouds the houses*
Unframe, the granite of the prime
Stand from the heaps: come storm and wash clean: the plaster is all
*   run to the sea and the steel*
All rusted; the foreland resumes
The form we loved when we saw it.   Though one at the end of the
*   age and far off from this place*
Should meet my presence in a poem,
The ghost would not care but be here, long sunset shadow in the
*   seams of the granite, and forgotten*
The flesh, a spirit for the stone.

It is all there, the basic attitude, Ossian's cleric-hating imprecation and Pound's resuscitated Seafarer, morosely grumbling
against the house-loving burgher and his bland ways. Going
through the poem I saw that it is not so much the ideas, it is
rather the mood, the feeling-toned attitude toward life and the

world, that is the motivating source. But I saw too that there is a purgation, that once more the poet is deep in his "heroic tribal role as purifier of the language," taking speech down to its pre-rational deeps and rubbing it clean upon psychic formations as grave and enduring as the stone beneath the coastal headland, and the elemental sea.

III

Elemental as it is, however, that mood is not established by a blind plunge to unconsciousness itself. The earth-man has his disciplines, though they may not be those of "clarity and pre-cision and vigor." As Rosenthal said of the technique behind Pound's Seafarer, "He makes certain repetitions of consonants and phrasing that the original does not have, to stress the func-tion of the alliteration as a major structural aspect of the Old English poem's rhythm." Jeffers too has his disciplines. He too, approaching the primordial sources, does so by a series of con-taining devices, in order that the purifying agents may operate, and that certain compelling indistinctions be permitted their way. But that such a way is carefully contained in a texture of profound emotional restraint and sustainment I hope to be able to show.

And that the attempt is overdue I cannot doubt. Squires writes: "The poems need critical re-examination, but the need centers in their philosophical texture, in the relationship of idea to idea rather than the relationship of word to word, nuance to nuance." It is my belief that the reverse is true. When R. P. Blackmur rejects what he calls "the flannel-mouthed inflation in the metric of Robinson Jeffers with his rugged rock-garden violence," no amount of ideational explication will appease him. He is a man for whom the only æsthetic norms are those of "clarity and precision and vigor"; and until it is demonstrated that there are other norms, and that their uses are vital to the life and well-being of language and hence of civilization, he will remain unconvinced. Word to word and nuance to nuance, then, for better or for worse, must be the attempt.

The poem begins directly, a terse declarative statement: "Happy people die whole." It is strangely reminiscent of the initial sentence of Tolstoy's *Anna Karenina*: "Happy families are all alike; every unhappy family is unhappy in its own way." Despite the time lag between them, that both are contemporary texts is shown by Joseph Campbell's mournful observation:

> With these fateful words, Count Leo Tolstoy opened the novel of the spiritual dismemberment of his modern heroine, Anna Karenina. During the seven decades that have elapsed since that distracted wife, mother and blindly impassioned mistress threw herself beneath the wheels of the train — thus terminating, with a gesture symbolic of what already had happened to her soul, her tragedy of disorientation — a tumultuous and unremitting dithyramb of romances, news reports, and unrecorded cries of anguish has been going up....Modern romance, like Greek tragedy, celebrates the mystery of dismemberment, which is life in time. The happy ending is justly scorned as a misrepresentation; for the world, as we know it, as we have seen it, yields but one ending: death, disintegration, dismemberment, and the crucifixion of our heart with the passing of the forms that we have loved.

If happy people are all alike in that they die whole, the family of man in our time is inconsolably unhappy in its own unique way.

Thus everything in Jeffers' opening line, like that of Tolstoy's, is preparational of what is to come. Each carries its force by a direct redundancy back upon the living texture of contemporary life. Already, in the poem, rhetoric is at work. Look first to the metric: this initial clause is composed of three feet: two trochees and a spondee:

Happy | *people* | *die whole*

The processive syllabization is taking us directly and inevitably into conceptual areas of subsistent moral consequence.

For the trochee, of course, is a falling foot, called so for obvious reasons, but its full value is prophetic. Its use is not exhausted in a material descent in emphasis. It *brings value down.* So here the trochees step down to instruct. But that the spondee takes a stand to reassure is no less evident: "die whole" has all the resolution of a sustained finality.

Four terse words, then, held together by three series of alliteration, the *h* sounds, the *p* sounds and the *e* sounds, of which the *y* in *happy* is one. Below that the operative force is in the vowel-progression: *a,e,i,o.* It is this elementary sequence that the alliteration cements and binds together. The progress is upwards in tonality, *a,e,i.* In the word *die* the progression reaches its apex, to be all resolved in the totality of the inclusive evocative word *whole. Happy people* was multi-syllabic, superficially dancing and gay in its insouciant lightness. (Clearly the poet somehow despises happy people.)*Die whole* pulls it in. It breaks it but resolves it. The clause stands complete. Out of the poet's unconscious, a man who knows he is not going to die whole because he is not a happy person, the need and the disbelief stand declared. We wait for clarification. It is a convincing opening, and a portentous one.

Such, then, clearly discernible in the first four words of the poem, are a few of the ingredients of Jeffers' basic rhetoric. So presented, it will not be necessary to dismantle every phrase, a process tedious and hardly to the point. It is only necessary to have established that what Blackmur has called "flannel-mouthed inflation" (*in the metric,* be it noted) is capable of the severest gravity and dignity. Not that Jeffers' style remains this tight. There are many among his contemporaries who will specialize in that till they glut it, tightness peddled till it drugs the market, but this man's method presumes otherness. As we go on we will see something of what it is, something of its enormous suggestibility, and why it is permitted, and why nothing less will suffice.

This looseness, this expansiveness that prefigures suggestibility, begins at once, but it is important to remind the reader
that it is as much a typographical looseness, a purely visual configuration, as a syllabic one. After the opening declaration we
get its issue: why happy people die whole. Because "they are all
dissolved in a moment," because "they have had what they
wanted," and because life has given them "no hard gifts." The
saints die spontaneously. So ripe in divine grace have they become, completely fulfilled and amplified in the potentialities of
life, that they seem to explode into heaven, vanishing without
a trace of regret into the tremendous Beatitude for which they
have offered up their lives. Whatever time brought them in the
way of adversity, they had so completely transmitted it into the
purposefulness to which they were committed that in the throes
of martyrdom itself they ecstatically proclaimed that truly they
owned to "no hard gifts." Jeffers clearly does not conceive of
himself as one of these.

But he does envy them. Here again the rhetoric tells us so —
"they are all dissolved in a moment," the deep gasp of fulfillment, the slaking of desire, in the long-syllabled "all dissolved."
Then the sage, idiomatic savoring, almost homely in its factu-
ality: "they have had what they wanted." How enviously the
folk mind relishes the fortune of others, whether it be in wealth
or in grace or in natural wisdom; then the short, terse smack of
satisfaction: "no hard gifts."

And once again the metric confirms it: these are largely anapests — always, from time immemorial, the accents of slaking
desire:

They are all | dissolved | in a moment

they have had | what they wanted

no hard gifts

Notice how the tri-stress, the mollossus, at the close rounds out the unit just as the spondee did the initial clause; only here, rather than the stable landing of "die whole," we get rather the light, most delicately accented laying on of the finger, like the touching of a healing wand: "no hard gifts."

Jeffers is content to let these vocables extend themselves across the page; he is groping out for his essential rhythm, endeavoring to discover what he is going to do about this matter in the lines ahead. He could have played it close. He could have enjambed the line on what is now a cæsura, brought everything in snug and short, shunted the ideograms back upon themselves to support his syllabic effect with a visual one, and ended with the look of tightness and control:

> Happy people die whole, they are all
> Dissolved in a moment; they have had
> What they wanted: no hard gifts.
> > The unhappy
> Linger a space, but pain
> Is a thing that is glad to be forgotten.

But it isn't that kind of poem. He is groping for the substance of a different mood, something less taut, less restrictive. This is not Lucretius meditating on the foibles of man; this is Ossian, fumbling about him in his profound discontent, hardly knowing whether to resist or succumb, suspiciously indicting the infiltration of hostile creeds, but half seduced by the mildness and flattery of the invader. He feels time and history are against him and he is not able to precipitate any *Götterdämmerung*. But on the other hand he does not intend to be convinced by luxuries, whether physical or metaphysical, and so he lets out his line to accommodate the ambivalence of his mood, sullen, taciturn, suspicious, unrepentant. It is the voice of the unconvinced, the wakeful, not-to-be-bilked, disaster-prone heart of man.

So happy people die whole, bursting with joy, and vanish in heaven. On the other hand are the disconsolate:

> the unhappy
> Linger a space, but pain is a thing that is glad to be forgotten.

These unsatisfied ones cannot depart with such ease, for there was a great deal of life they did not voluntarily renounce. The joy they craved in this world was denied them, and thus they linger, but only for a space, for pain is indeed a thing that is glad to be forgotten. However, there remains a third degree of irresolution, and this is spiritual, ideational:

> but one who has given
> His heart to a cause or a country,
> His ghost may spaniel it awhile, disconsolate to watch it.

The great patriots and the great reformers, breaking themselves on the hopeless imperviousness of the human heart, die neither spiritually ripe nor psychologically maimed, but yet with a kind of dissident unfulfillment. Such a lingering may be seen in his poem "Woodrow Wilson," written earlier, and may be seen again in the more negatively delineated "The Dead to Clemenceau," coming a year or two later on.

But Jeffers does not consider himself as belonging to any of these three categories. The possibility of a painful death he had just considered in a companion piece, "Ante Mortem," but his grouping of the three irresolutions together here indicates he has as yet no real prospect of that. What does he expect or predict for himself? It is the answer to this question which is indeed the substance of his poem, but before we proceed let us stop the loom and look a bit at the fabric, for within its rhetorical texture will already have been determined the kind of stuff this cloth will prove to be.

IV

Jeffers, in these few lines, sketches out, succinctly but emphatically, conceptual substance enough to make an entire poem, if he were inclined to have it so. But because he has not wanted to let it go at quite that he governs his material in this stricter way. We find, for instance, the phrases do not extend out and envelop the whole of the possibilities latent in the ideational nucleus. Sensing involvement in no more than provisional attitudes he keeps his measure in check. It is this fact, this keeping in check, which permits us to see something of his handling of the larger rhythmic unit, the vehicular phrase.

For every technical device is nothing more than the key to an attitude, and in poetry attitude is all. The shift in point of view of Western man since the Renaissance has resulted in a gradual abandonment of traditional metrical structures and a rise in the development of prose style to carry the conscience of the race. In prose style set syllabic regularity is relaxed, the uniform measure of line is dispersed, and something more variable, the idiomatic phrase, emerges as the organizing implement of emotive force. The poetic revolution of 1912 was introduced largely to accommodate into poetry the resilience of what had become an incontrovertible fact, the primacy of prose sensibility, and this was first done via the movement called *vers libre*. But *vers libre* as practiced was too light to accommodate the more grave and imponderable uses that poetry traditionally has borne. A verse form begotten of the cultural opulence of the prewar period, an era characterized by an exclusion of conscience in material satisfaction, the glutting of instinct in sensual commodities, was quite unable to sustain the terrible burden of the world's most awesome conflict. At any rate, the traditionalists, fronting a postwar chaos localized in the spasm of indictive cynicism, soon cut back toward the measured norm. We see it clearly in Eliot. As an experimentalist, under the tutelage of Pound he had created Experimentalism's masterpiece, *The Waste Land*, only to cut back sharply to traditionalism. Even in *The Waste Land* the formalist latencies were lurking. Twenty years later Robert Lowell, cresting on Eliot's long traditionalist triumph, could detect, in no more than four lines of that masterpiece, the nucleus of a formalist idiom, and perfect that idiom into a dominant style:

> *And each man fixed his eyes before his feet.*
> *Flowed up the hill and down King William Street,*
> *To where Saint Mary Woolnoth kept the hours*
> *With a dead sound . . .*

And what of Experimentalism, the breakthrough movement that precipitated modernist verse? Why did it crumble at last before the traditionalist attack? That is a long and complex story, contingent upon two world wars, a global depression, the assimilation of all spontaneous revolutionary *élan* in competing power structures — in a word, "the routinization of the charismatic." But one thing is certain: the solution of Whitman, who had antedated *vers libre* by sixty years, was not utilized to any degree by the technical innovators, and hence the tremendous vitality of his achievement went by the board. Pound's acknowledgement of him was too ambivalent to be efficacious. It was the matter of his relaxed idiom. Pound and the *vers librists*, as we noted, wanted a more explicitly precisionist method, a more strict and conscious control. Whitman, like Blake before and D. H. Lawrence after him (technically the three shakiest major poets in the language) depended upon another mode of shaping. In Lawrence's words, which will serve as well for the others, "I have always tried to get an emotion on its own course without altering it. It needs the finest instinct imaginable, much finer than the skill of the craftsman." But as a skill, that kind of instinct is notoriously unreliable, and an ambitious man like

Pound was not going to stake his all on anything so indeterminate.

Nor, actually, would Jeffers. Jeffers knew what Lawrence meant, certainly, and probably believed it in his bones, but he would never have acknowledged the dictum for himself. He was trained in Greek by the age of five, and though intuitively requiring the same psychic equivalent as the relatively unschooled Whitman, he found the solutions of the Good Gray Poet too disingenuously obvious, too transparently *available*, for his classical formation, his reserved aristocratic instinct, to accept utterly. In the end, however, more than any other American, he was able to profit by those exhilarating innovations without debasing them, without, that is, succumbing to the lure of such accidentals as invested them, and he did it by thoroughly masking the abiding presence under his own prosodic system. This masking was so astute it concealed his debt even from himself.

Nor is it unnatural that Jeffers denied the influence of Whitman. He sensed a threat. Alberts writes:

> It has been the fashion, among the members of the glib-phrase-making school of criticism in this country and in England, to criticise R.J. in terms of Walt Whitman. The practice is, of course, absurd, and had these "critics" looked beyond the superficial similarity of irregular, unrhymed printed lines, they would possibly have noticed the essentially dissimilar philosophy contained therein. As for W. W.'s influence on R. J., Una Jeffers writes that: *R. J. says he owes less to W. W. than to most other poets of his era and sees no reason to link W. W. and R. J.*

The historic contiguity of the two American giants, however, is too evident to be doubted. Both in cosmic outlook and in originality of style they stand shoulder to shoulder, or rather back to back, since they look in opposite directions. What Jeffers owes to Whitman is the very thing Lawrence spoke of: "the instinct to get an emotion on its own course without altering

it." This was Whitman's great intuitive gift and all poets of
the open style are immeasurably in his debt. For instance, Jeffers' capacity to tap an emotion springing directly from nature:

> *Westward the wave-gleaners,*
> *The old gray sea-going gulls are gathered together, the north-west*
>   *wind wakening*
> *Their wings to the wild spirals of the wind-dance.*
> *Fresh as the air, salt as the foam, play birds in the bright wind, fly*
>   *falcons*
> *Forgetting the oak and the pinewood, come gulls*
> *From the Carmel sands and the sands at the river-mouth, from Lobos*
>   *and out of the limitless*
> *Power of the mass of the sea, for a poem*
> *Needs multitude, multitudes of thoughts, all fierce, all flesh-eaters,*
>   *musically clamorous*
> *Bright hawks that hover and dart headlong, and ungainly*
> *Gray hungers fledged with desire of transgression,*
>   *salt slimed beaks, from the sharp*
> *Rock-shores of the world and the secret waters.*

This is unmistakably Jeffers, but the marvelous sensitivity of
questing emotion, the breath-taking unfurling of intuition (not
in terms of stylistic derivation, but of creative attitude), the
capacity to drop the guard and launch out in absolute trust to
pure internality, unconscious stimulus localized in the registration of nature in language itself, is directly derived from
Whitman:

> *You sea! I resign myself to you also — I guess what you mean,*
> *I behold from the beach your crooked inviting fingers,*
> *I believe you refuse to go back without feeling of me,*
> *We must have a turn together, I undress, hurry me out of sight of*
>   *the land,*
> *Cushion me soft, rock me in billowy drowse,*
> *Dash me with amorous wet, I can repay you.*
> *Sea of stretch'd ground-swells,*
> *Sea breathing broad and convulsive breaths,*

Sea of the brine of life and of unshovell'd yet always-ready graves,
Howler and scooper of storms, capricious and dainty sea,
I am integral with you, I too am of one phase and of all phases.

If we can say without exaggeration that craftsmanship is the oarsman's skill, then it goes without saying that Walt invented the surfboard.

As for Jeffers, he found his solution to the problem of the two needs within him (the need of tradition as the "ought" and of inspiration as the "is,") by scanning his verse not metrically but quantitatively in the Greek way. Because some system of scansion was in play his classical conscience was salved, the regularity of quantitative stress imposed on the lines gave them the look of limit, a typography that suggested, vaguely, an inner freedom within an ordered whole. Discounting the fact that there can be no real equivalence between the two languages, quantity unnaturally applied to English allowed him the latitude to organize the generative force of his genius and at the same time meet his classical requirements. In my attempts to analyze, to comprehend the basic Jeffersian idiom, I was never convinced by this device, which I came to accept as an author's stratagem necessary to keep the two sides of his nature in play. No more was I convinced by Hopkins' "sprung rhythm" and for the same reason. I suspected two Greek scholars loyal to the great tradition, obliged to present their credentials as guarantors of their technical orthodoxy, but driven by the creative force of their genius to *de facto* heresy. For the real operative source in the case of both Jeffers and Hopkins does not depend on consistency of metric. That metric is sacrificed at any given point to the actual force of language which is proceeding by virtue of something larger, more inclusive. In *A Dictionary of Literary Terms* we read:

> Meter produces *rhythm*, recurrences at equal intervals, but rhythm (from a Greek word meaning "flow") is usually applied to larger

units than feet. Often it depends most obviously on pauses. Thus, a poem with run-on lines will have a different rhythm from a poem with end-stopped lines, even though both are in the same meter. And prose, though it is unmetrical, can thus have rhythm too. In addition to being affected by syntactical pauses, rhythm is affected by pauses due to consonant clusters and the length of words. Polysyllabic words establish a different rhythm from monosyllabic words, even in metrically identical lines. One can say, then, that rhythm is altered by shifts in meter, syntax, and the length and ease of pronunciation. But even with no such shift, even if a line is repeated verbatim, a reader may sense a change in rhythm.

It seemed to me that both Jeffers and Hopkins adopted equivocal systems (quantity in the one case, sprung rhythm in the other) in order to have it both ways, for that was their need, honoring the normative tradition by employing an identifiable "system" they could point to, at the same time retaining the artist's inalienable right to sacrifice that system, shift the weight from *metric*, whenever the interior line of creative energy decreed it, to *rhythm*. And it also seemed to me that if that was all that was necessary to get the poetry out, then bless the self-deception. It was little enough to pay.

For one can forgive an artist, as Jeffers forgave Nature, "a thousand graceful subtleties," the act of creation being necessarily cozened from the soul by a host of deployments, or only one, according to a man's need. But we ought not fracture our minds in an effort to make practice conform to theory at every implausible point. In prosody, which is certainly relative, unlike theology, which must be absolute, heresy can be more than the spice of life; it may well be its gut, muscle and semen. Theology can tolerate no more heresy than the intriguing stimulus needed to spur it on to essentials. And though many in both disciplines have no such care (the real rebels always walk away from the problem entirely) there remain those complex souls, intransigently orthodox in spirit, in whom subsists such a powerful instinct for heresy that they are impelled to create whole systems of defiant genius, as we see in the case of an Arian and a Luther, each of whom, radically heretical, contrived an orthodoxy out of political adventitiousness to veil the discrepancy, and dominated their age. So in art the absolute necessity to find unfettered modes in order to get the draught of the burgeoning unconscious, powerful in revolt, out and operative, can adopt the guise of a deceptive traditionalism. Thus Jeffers. And in his case the prosodic orthodoxy, given his adroitness, was beautifully deceptive. When the powerful rhythms began to commit mayhem on the vulnerable public psyche of the twenties, it was a sign that something unprecedented, something terribly primitive yet strangely sophisticated, was irresistibly in play.

At any rate, when I early came to the problem of Jeffers' prosody, it was apparent to me that the rhythm, the underlying driving force, was going on at a fundamentally different level from the rationale. Quantitative prosody? On the contrary, something ineluctable was at work, and it stemmed, as I have said, inherently in elements more inclusive than any consideration of metrics, elements appropriated from what had developed as essentially prose devices. I saw it as something centered upon a relationship of phrase to phrase, and in order to verify this insight, I broke down Jeffers' poem to its phraseological components, seeking to lay bare the secret of the force, to bring it out where it could be identified:

> Happy people die whole
> they are all dissolved in a moment
> they have had what they wanted
> no hard gifts.
> The unhappy linger a space
> but pain is a thing that is glad to be forgotten.
> But one who has given his heart to a cause or a country
> his ghost may spaniel it awhile
> disconsolate to watch it.

Considered visually, judging the work solely as it appears under the eye, a radically different kind of poem emerges from the one we felt it to have been when we first saw it in Jeffers' original typography. That Jeffers did not want this look, this impression, this predispositional configuration, leading to some unavoidable interpretation of his content, is evident from the fact that he did not print it in any such fashion. And yet, so reconstructed, we can see his actual use of phrasing to check and contain material that could have been expanded to make a substantial poem. By the almost reluctant containment of phraseological possibility he prevents himself from prematurely losing sight of his main attempt, which was to disemburden himself of something radically different from these provisional ideas, yet which is itself an emotional extension of them. The poetry, outside the one fine figure of the ghost doting on its past as a spaniel fawns on a master, subsists in the contained potentiality of the larger rhythms. That the looseness is something indigenous to the principal mood , which is yet to be developed but must not be allowed to become too strict, is indicated by the repetition of the word "but," a repetition suggesting an air of curious ineffectuality, like the ghost ruminating upon its unchangeable past. (I see in my mind his figure of King Arthur, in the later poem "Ghosts in England," pathetically handling the sword Excalibur.) That carelessly repeated "but," which from an explicitly conscious consideration of verse-craft, some might fault as a lapse, operates in the general dulling, obscuring effect, the fumbling, crumbling impression of the inexplicit.

I have strayed a bit from my main purpose in breaking the lines down, which was to establish the larger element in Jeffersian rhetoric, the handling of the phrase. In this introduction we have three groups of phrases, two threes (I judge the "no hard gifts" to be actually an outrider from the previous phrase) separated by one group of two.

> *Happy people die whole*
> 3   *they are all dissolved in a moment*
> *they have had what they wanted*
> *no hard gifts.*

> 2   *The unhappy linger a space*
> *but pain is a thing that is glad to be forgotten.*

> *But one who has given his heart to a cause or a country*
> 3   *his ghost may spaniel it awhile*
> *disconsolate to watch it.*

This three-two-three variation is the essence of the larger unitary formal pattern of the opening and it is effective. Notice how the lengths of these phrases are set in tension one against the other, the inner dynamic of all free verse, substituting an asymmetrical juxtaposition for the symmetrical regularity of blank verse.

The first group are short, they pick themselves up on each other rather lightly, the blitheness, shall we say, of "the happy" caught up and stressed just sufficiently to establish the point without making too much of it, and the little sub-phrase *no hard gifts* extending the line, like the final, almost happy upreach of a wave sliding in and out of the surf, a kind of lip of foam: the last reach:

> *Happy people die whole*
> *they are all dissolved in a moment*
> *they have had what they wanted: no hard gifts.*

The middle group simply establishes the opposite, the counterpart in the ideational dialectic, so two phrases suffice, the last line being the longest we have encountered, going right on out to the end. Notice too the cæsura after "unhappy," the unavoidable cessation that separates it from the haunting word "linger." That "unhappy" picks up the "no hard gifts," the lip from the preceding sequence, and breaks it ever so slightly:

> *The unhappy / linger a space*
> *But pain is a thing that is glad to be forgotten.*

How well the anapests serve here, lengthening, extending. And
yet never letting go; we are never to forget that this is simply
the preamble, though in the opening line of the last sequence we
have the longest push so far permitted us:

> *But one who has given his heart to a cause or a country.*

Here the metric is anapest, but not so uniformly exemplified as
in the preceding line. There is a blurring, a softening of focus,
the beat is more slurred. It needs perhaps the recognition of a
cæsura after "one" to bring it into strictness:

> *But one / who has given his heart to a cause or a country.*

And rhythmically this is the tidecrest, the longest reach; two
containing phrases bring the line down to a termination, and
the preamble is over.

Other elements than rhythmic ones are at work to establish
the tone. Not only does the final third give the only figure of
the passage, the powerful word *spaniel* as a verb to catch up the
worrisome nature of the fascination with the past, but the un-
grammatical "but one...his ghost" serves to establish again the
lack of strictness of the mood aborning, its colloquial earthiness,
and the wonderfully evocative word "disconsolate" to richen
the entire figure. The tone is grave, deliberate, and hence dig-
nified, all in keeping with the tenor of the matter at hand, Death
and Transfiguration. The overall influence of alliteration in
achieving this degree of complicity and evocation will be
touched on later.

In subjecting these lines to such detailed analysis, it has not
been my endeavor to prove that they are intrinsically great
verse. The poem is great; from this point forward the lines will

become very great indeed, but so far that greatness exists largely *in potentia*. I have endeavored only to demonstrate that while it is true Jeffers is a poet of direct statements, he is also a master rhetorician, and that it is precisely by the authority of his rhetoric that he lifts his statements, merely provisional statements, into consequentiality. Direct statement is the vehicle of fact, whether phenomenal fact or ideational fact, but rhetoric is the vehicle of consequentiality. It is in rhetoric that the implicative value of fact is established in depth, and it is, in the last resort, to rhetoric alone that we look for ultimate meanings. That Jeffers has been able to take matter that is patently preparational and, in stating it, endow it with the gravity, the somberness, the requisite saliency, preserving it from the superficial and the transitory, is an achievement of rhetoric, and it is superb.

V

We arrive, then, at the main body of the poem, for which Jeffers has been denying himself the not inconsiderable temptation to develop his three categories of the dying, for they are in themselves quite intriguing, and would doubtless afford many interesting observations. It is true that happy people who die whole have little interest for him; but for what he might have done with the unhappy whose pain is glad to be forgotten we must wait till Margrave's son's death. As for those who have given their heart to a cause or a country, he has just touched on that, as we saw, in "Woodrow Wilson." What he is trying for now is something of far greater cruciality, for he introduced his categories only because he realized that he does not fit into them. What he has to find out is something about himself.

> *. . . I was wondering how long the spirit*
> *That sheds this verse will remain*
> *When the nostrils are nipped, when the brain rots in its vault*
> *or bubbles in the violence of fire*
> *To be ash in metal.*

Now the poet is engaged. I was wondering, he says, almost casually, how long the spirit that *sheds* this verse will remain. Mark the verb. There is a note of contempt in that, coupled with the casualness of his wondering, as if all the high idealism of his youth had been corrupted by the millions who died in the wind-rows of Flanders, like fallen leaves. Trees shed leaves; we will recall it later on. Bodies shed garments, and the soul worries its garment like a spaniel worries a rag. The same pinch of death that nips the shed leaves now nips the nostrils of the man who one day must die, and the splendid mind of man, the seat of the soul, becomes a putridness, rots in its "vault" ("why lay ye up treasure on earth that moth can corrupt?") and bubbles with the violence of fire. In both "sheds" and "bubbles" we catch the irony of the contradiction between man's pride and his mani-fest fate. Notice the two latent cæsuræ, one behind "wonder-ing" and the other behind "brain," to check and hence enforce the savage impulsion in the mind that strikes in its irony at its own impermanence.

> *I was wondering*
> *how long the spirit that sheds this verse will **remain***
> *when the nostrils are nipped*
> *when the brain*
> *rots in its vault*
> *or bubbles in the violence of fire*
> *to be ash in metal.*

Observe particularly how the cæsura behind "brain" gives the strong verb "rots" its heightened impact. Notice too how the use of the word "violence" gives a whipping, flame-like quality to enforce the seethe already instituted by "bubbles," and the soft collapse of all in "to be ash in metal." But that soft collapse can never suffice as resolution. The ironic mind has just tasted blood. Not to be denied, the poet now pushes downward to an-other level of the unconscious. In the repetitive, declarative phrases the mere wonderment, caught up again, becomes real through, and the impulsion drives down:

> *Some stalks of the wood whose roots I married to the earth*
> *   of this place will stand five centuries;*
> *I held the roots in my hand,*
> *The stems of the trees between two fingers.*

In this secondary imagery we have, in truth, approached what is disturbing the poet, and by extension, ourselves. For we have touched, ever so lightly, the erotic root of our problem. He describes the act of planting by the word "married." The phallic symbolism is given a kind of incipient delicacy in the three words, "stalks," "roots," and "stems." Jeffers said that he planted 2000 trees, eucalyptus and cypress, on the headland where he lived, to shield his house from the encroachment of suburbia. In a powerful seizure of the imagination the poet perceives the magnificent trunks of the future trees held nascent between his two fingers, and the symbol works into the problem of the transience of life which is here his underlying theme.

But this is primarily erotic symbolism. Marriage is the act of procreation. The sexuality of planting has been amply documented by both anthropologists and psychologists, and the association between the rotation of the crops and the fertility rites is well known. Here it is operating not in a mythical (collective) but in a psychological (individual) dimension. But before we go on to what it gives place to, let us look at that texture a bit, to instruct ourselves in what the *libido*, the life force, is doing in its search for outlet.

> *I was thinking*
> *some stalks of the wood whose roots I married to the earth of this place*
> *will stand five centuries.*
> *I held the roots in my hand*
> *the stems of the trees between two fingers.*

The parallelism of "I was wondering" and "I was thinking" are matched also by the long phrases that follow them. Here the long inching out of the second phrase is very significant. Not only does it balance the secondary phrase of the preceding passage, but the psyche seems involved in a root-like inching out, a quest for its center of disturbance. Notice also how the two final phrases work to pull back that inching out, contain it. There is, too, a contrapuntal interplay of prime words: *stalks, roots, roots, stems.* There are two concealed rhymes: *stand-hand, I-my.* There is much primary alliteration: *was, wood, will; stalks, stand, stems; 'tween, two; married, my; held, hand; five, fingers.* There is secondary alliteration: *stems, trees, 'tween, two; thinking, the, earth, this, the, the, the.*

But when we restore the double passage to its original typography, we see that the analytical breakdown of phrases overemphasizes their division, and that what actually emerges out of the totality is a kind of hurrying, as when a man hastens on to something of great consequence to him, driven more by inner motivation than by any object he has fastened upon, but irregularly hurrying forward into the destiny which he intuits is there, so that his broken progression takes on a kind of dance-like impulsion.

> I was wondering how long the spirit
> That sheds this verse will remain
> When the nostrils are nipped, when the brain rots in
>   its vault or bubbles in the violence of fire
> To be ash in metal. I was thinking
> Some stalks of the wood whose roots I married
>   to the earth of this place will stand five centuries.
> I held the roots in my hand,
> The stems of the trees between two fingers.

Nor do I want to hear anyone say that such a shambling, or even dancelike progression, is not appropriate to the material of this text; for certainly the unconscious, when it quickens toward its term, takes on a profoundly different character of rhythm than an objective disposition of its conscious material might signify, and it is part of the business of analysis to separate the two currents.

So we have hurried forward in our unconscious progression, more like a rivulet indeed than like a dance, and now at last we burst out upon the substance of what was disturbing us, and what all our vegetative and womb (vault) symbolism was compelling us toward. We have arrived, that is to say, at the unabashed, uncontainable, and yes, the imagery denotes it, the disgusting primacy of female sexuality:

> ... *how many remote generations of women*
> *Will drink joy from men's loins.*

It is strange how the word "remote" here is made to serve the uses of imprisonment, serving both to detach the poet from involvement in the irregularities he disdains and to specify the extent of its prolongation in time: an infinite succession of aggressive female sexual acts, terrifying the masculine mind with its weak hold on rationality and spiritual balance. Yet threatened though we are by this eventuality we are unable to deny the libido its great slaking efficacy, the indubitable vitality of sexual gratification: "Drink joy," the poet says, gasping, "from men's loins"! The rich biblical evocativeness of the sexual implication of "loins" fuses with the phallic jabbing of the syllables; generations, drink, joy. And out of this awesome mindlessness the terrible consequences, the brute unstaunchable evacuation of the womb:

> *And dragged from between the thighs of what mothers will*
> *giggle at my ghost.*

Everything about the line reveals that we have arrived at the heart of the poet's unconscious disturbance. The unrelenting mechanism of birth and the haunting fear of insanity conjoin in those terrible verbs: "dragged" and "giggle." Between their inexorable vitality already they have done for the man, and he "gives up the ghost." This symbol of failure finds voice immediately, turns against the phallicism of life as it "curses the axemen," and collapses back into the diaphanous figures of capitulation, "Gray impotent voice on the sea-wind," to hover over the ultimate image of castration: "when the last trunk falls." Here, of course, the vegetative symbolism of roots, stalks, stems and now trunks, retains a residual faith in instinctual life, while the axemen symbolize man's corrupt, ego-centric aggressiveness.

But what is the agent of man's aggressiveness? Civilization. And who is the author of civilization? "In the deeps of his imagery," someone has said, "the poet cannot lie." It is out of such depths that Jeffers points the accusing finger at the one culprit: Woman. She it was who seduced man in his primal beginnings. She it is for whom man labors in bondage, her slave, creating and sustaining a world of sensuality and pleasure, triviality and merely material proficiency. In the same anguish of soul the author of the Apocalypse had cried out:

> So he carried me away in the spirit into the wilderness: and I saw a woman sit upon a scarlet colored beast, full of names of blasphemy, having seven heads and ten horns. And the woman was arrayed in purple and scarlet color, and decked with gold and precious stones and pearls, having a golden cup in her hand full of abominations and filthiness of her fornication: and upon her forehead was a name written, MYSTERY, BABYLON THE GREAT, THE MOTHER OF HARLOTS AND ABOMINATIONS OF THE EARTH. And I saw the woman drunken with the blood of the saints, and with the blood of the martyrs of Jesus: and when I saw her, I wondered with great admiration.

All this fascination and disgust Jeffers catches up in a single
concept: Abundance.

> The women's abundance will have built
> roofs over all this foreland;
> Will have buried the rock foundations
> I laid here.

But having evoked woman as the symbol of hectic, phrenetic
sexuality, of civilization, frivolity and stultifying domesticity,
the poet has arrived at one of the most profound dilemmas of
the psyche: behind the images of the destructive woman lies the
more primal image of woman as beneficent Nature, the Great
Mother of cosmic being. It is this complexity, this complication
that confuses the clear masculine spirit, and renders it unable to
declare itself unequivocally for the simple solution. This is why
the poet, having failed in his effort to stave off involvement,
having set one feminine symbol against another, set instinct
against eroticism, and unconscious freedom against domesticity, grave dignity against fickle frivolity, cannot extricate
himself from the hopelessness of inconclusive choice, and must
see at last frivolity triumph, the trees of instinctual nature cut
down by the bastard sons of the errant daughters of the Mother.

But below the hopelessness of that choice, below the implacable mechanism of maternal reproductivity or the nympho-
mania of erotic stimulation, he has recourse to something she
cannot corrupt, and this is stone. Stone, the ancient symbol of
integrity and spiritual essence, of the permanent and the abiding, which the hectic activity of woman can bury but never
deplete. Stone emerges as the symbol of salvation, and in the
permanence of that substance

> the women's exuberance will canker and fail in its time

the long line rolling out to the final cancellation of all his trouble.
To canker and fail is the punishment she richly deserves for

her provocative blandishments, her errant eroticism, as Isaiah
warned so many centuries earlier:

> *Because the daughters of Zion are haughty,*
> *And walk with stretched forth necks and wanton eyes,*
> *Walking and mincing as they go,*
> *And making a tinkling with their feet:*
> *Therefore the Lord will smite with a scab*
> *The crown of the head of the daughters of Zion,*
> *And the Lord will discover their secret parts . . .*

And in this certitude the righteous judgment of the prophet's
heir, the beleaguered poet, afflicted by his rebellious senses and
praying deliverance, rides out to the great denouement, a chop-
ping, rocking death-dance of final cancellation:

> *and like clouds the houses*
> *Unframe, the granite of the prime*
> *Stand from the heaps.*

In the impetuosity of expectation the poet cannot wait; he
moves back from the future tense to the present one:

> *come storm and wash clean: the plaster is all run to the sea*
> *and the steel*
> *All rusted.*

Until at last the sin of egocentric female excess is annulled in a
divine purgation, and maternal nature restored to her original
simplicity:

> *the foreland resumes*
> *The form we loved when we saw it.*

It is done. The spasm of revulsion is over. Having found the
symbol of integration, satisfied that some destiny obtains beyond the cycle of death and rebirth, the poet can go into his
epilogue, restoring unto himself the deep and contained mood
of his prologue, with its evident satisfactions of finality and
arrival. In some profound way, too, he must feel that his poem,

having been rubbed on the permanence of rock, brings back to
life something of its timelessness, a sufficient immortality to
secure for him some portion of the future.

> *Though one at the end of the age*
>   *and far off from this place*
> *Should meet my presence in a poem,*
> *The ghost would not care but be here, long sunset shadow*
>   *in the seams of the granite, and forgotten*
> *The flesh, a spirit for the stone.*

VI

There is no need, in conclusion, for further analysis. The resolving cadences and conclusive rhetoric that bear toward finality
are self-evident, and they are magnificent. Everything carries
forward into the dark quietude, the abiding peace. Nor need
we be offended by the poet's withdrawal from our world. The
mystic and the visionary, for whom the twin aspects of woman
— eroticism and domesticity — are always a most vexatious
problem, from time immemorial have withdrawn into desert
places, fastening down for anchor upon the abiding symbols
of permanence in a world of flux. Today the visionary, the
artist, seeks solitude through his art as well, and if the solutions he proposes are not adequate to the whole needs of life, as
Jeffers' solutions seem hardly consonant with all that secular
humanity seeks for itself, nevertheless he serves immeasurably
in the integrity of his very attempt. Let his attempt, if not his
attainment, stay us against mortality.

For what the poet feels, and in feeling comprehends, is common to all men, though we may not be aware of it, and he
reveals our feelings in his own, so that we too may comprehend
them. It is not necessary to indict him for his candor. Hostility
to woman is archaic, but it is also archetypal — an ineradicable
factor in the masculine heart. Woe to the man who thinks it is

not so, or believes he has outlived it with his adolescence. The
fear of woman is essentially the fear of matter itself, the darkening of the intellect. The terror of the spirit trapped in the flesh,
never escaping the bond of nature, has inspired many great
religions with their key motifs of salvation through asceticism,
ultimate liberation from the Wheel of material being. Possibly
the early personal life of the poet is accountable for the closeness
of these problems to his conscious mind, but the *trauma*, the
symbolic wound that makes the artist what he is, can only activate archetypes subsistent in the race itself. Listen to Robert
Graves sketch the core of the compulsion:

> The Goddess is a lovely, slender woman with a hooked nose, deathly
> pale face, lips red as rowan-berries, startlingly blue eyes and long
> fair hair; she will suddenly transform herself into sow, mare, bitch,
> vixen, she-ass, weasel, serpent, owl, she-wolf, tigress, mermaid or
> loathsome hag. Her names and titles are innumerable. In ghost
> stories she often figures as "The White Lady," and in ancient reli-
> gions, from the British Isles to the Caucasus, as the "White God-
> dess." I cannot think of any true poet from Homer onwards who has
> not independently recorded his experience of her. The test of a poet's
> vision, one might say, is the accuracy of his portrayal of the White
> Goddess and of the island over which she rules. The reason why the
> hairs stand on end, the eyes water, the throat is constricted, the skin
> crawls and a shiver runs down the spine when one writes or reads
> a true poem is that a true poem is necessarily an invocation of the
> White Goddess, or Muse, the Mother of All Living, the ancient pow-
> er of fright and lust — the female spider or the queen-bee whose
> embrace is death. Housman offered a secondary test of true poetry:
> whether it matches a phrase of Keats's, "everything that reminds me
> of her goes through me like a spear." This is equally pertinent to the
> Theme. Keats was writing under the shadow of death about his
> Muse, Fanny Brawne; and the "spear that roars for blood" is the
> traditional weapon of the dark executioner and supplanter.

Jeffers himself has celebrated her under a score of forms: Tamar,
who drew her father and her brother and her lover to the upper

room and destroyed them with fire; Fera Martial, who wore the panther skin and tripped off the skein of events that sent Hood to his death and Cawdor to his blindness; California, who watched the stallion trample her man to pieces and then murdered God; Claire Walker, the eternal virgin whom childbirth must destroy; Helen Thurso, who betrayed her husband and cut his throat out of awe; Fayne Fraser, who seduced her brother-in-law and brought the curse down on the house; Gudrun, who "wanted her brothers killed . . . wanted, not wanted, gets what she wanted, and drinks a knife." Over and over Jeffers has sought to wring understanding by pleading that the world's violence was not his invention. "A man having bad dreams, who invents victims, is only the ape of God." Faithful to the primacy of man's immortal anguish, he has the supreme dignity to register our hostilities and our fears at their very root. He bares his wounds, indeed, but through the metaphor of his art, his wounds become our balm.

"It is the poet who protects the 'whole machinery of social and individual thought and order' against catastrophe through his heroic tribal role as purifier of the language." Taking his craft back to elemental sources he refurbishes our speech, returning to the underlying levels at which language was born, the prime responses of consciousness and oblivion, fear and survival, the imponderable mystery of what passes and what abides. In the purification ritual which is his act of creation we too can touch something of his search for cleanness, and by gazing with him into the pool of man's self confront our own hostilities, return to life fortified against them; for ours are his, as his are ours. Secretly understanding his resources, we are, in God's grace, momentarily delivered from the mordant extremity of his actual solutions.

4
The Beauty of God

A review, slightly expanded, of the posthumous
volume *The Beginning and the End.*
Published originally in *Ramparts*, Christmas, 1963,
it treats chiefly of Jeffers' power to retain
his vitality to the limit of his life, and touches
on the matter of his tendentiousness in general and
his antagonism to Christianity in particular.

> Respect humanity, Death, these
> shameless black eyes of yours,
> It is not necessary to take all at once—besides that, you
> cannot do it, we are too powerful . . .
> We have invented the jet-plane and the death-bomb and the
> cross of Christ—"Oh," he said, "surely
> You'll live forever"—grinning like a skull, covering his
> mouth with his hand—"What could exterminate you?"
> —Passenger Pigeons

Many strictures against Robinson Jeffers could be grouped under one: tendentiousness, perhaps the most condemned item in the critical index of our time. Our æsthetic reveres the pure essence; it is anti-polemical, anti-programmatic, basically anti-subject matter. For us, propagation is propaganda, and we disdain it. Nevertheless, there is a certain genre, actually a very powerfully genre, which is the direct product of the committed spirit, and a good case for the superiority of the English tradition in poetry can be made for it: the inflexible rectitude of its moral concern. And we do see this element deeply operative in Jeffers. In the mature work of his supreme middle years he hurled his indictments and asserted his pronouncements with pulverizing intensity. Now, in this last book of his life, assembled after his death by his sons and his literary executor, the tendentiousness persists, but it is more at the level of contemptuous rumination than of the original blazing asseveration.

Take, for instance, his well-known antipathy to Christianity. While not the main target of his indictment, it nevertheless figured everywhere in his work. He blighted his best poem with a puerile reference to "harps and habitations" behind the stars. The same animus is not absent from his final volume:

> That all men are born free and equal: consider that!
> And that a wandering Hebrew poet named Jesus
> Is the God of the universe. Consider that!

I seem to be back in my boyhood, behind the stove at the corner store, listening to the village atheist spit tobacco juice through the parson's Sunday sermon.

This anti-Christian hostility is, of course, not hard to account for, considering the era of his religious indoctrination: hard-

shell, arrogant, tail-of-the-century Old Testamentism locked in
a death-struggle with an equally arrogant, equally implacable
Darwinian scientism. Add to it a minister for father-figure, and
you have a Puller-Down-of-the-Gods of no mean potential.
Jeffers proved true to the form.

> *He is no God of love, no justice of a little city like Dante's Florence,*
>   *no anthropoid God*
> *Making commandments: this is the God who does not care and will*
>   *never cease . . .*

So he believed. And never realized that to speak of a God who
"does not care" is about as "anthropoid" as you can get.

For it can not be denied that, despite himself, Jeffers' attitude
contained powerful residual Christian elements. Chief of these
was his view of mankind isolated from the divine and fastened
upon itself, inbreeding to its own vitiation and destruction.
Jeffers' indictment of civilization was one the early Christians
would have understood completely, however thoroughly contemporary ones are scandalized by the totality of such rejection.
He is surely one of the great poets of Original Sin, a matter that
should have made him fashionable with certain latter-day es-
thetes. But he did not register his concern with the consolatory
cultural finesse of, say, an Eliot. What Jeffers saw, not as a
stimulating dash of cultural bitters, but with appalling clarity,
was that mankind has turned its back upon the vision of God,
and in consequence, like a disemboweled hyena chonking down
its own viscera, is consuming itself as it dies. True, Jeffers saw
this God not as Jehovah but as Nature, but he saw that, Nature
or Jehovah, the outcome is the same. He saw that only a humanity which contemplates unremittingly the divine Otherness can
be whole, can maintain wholeness; that a humanity turned from
contemplation inevitably becomes obsessed with itself, not as
consumes itself insatiably, imprisoned in the ghastly quicksilver
Other but as Only, a face in the mirror, and in this obsession

of complacency, licentiousness and violence. In this sense his vision was profoundly Christian, whatever else it was. Nor does his pantheism throw him among the oriental mystics, nor any contemporaneous fashionable version thereof. In "On an Anthology of Chinese Poems" he complains, "But why do their rocks have no weight?" and asks, "It is a moral difference perhaps?"

It is, indeed. For morality is the mode of the distinct Ego, seeing itself opposite the Other as an independent agent of knowledge and will. No, the subsistent Christianity of Robinson Jeffers, or rather his Old Testamentish reduction of it, runs too deep and ineradicable through all his verse to be discounted. A man cannot extirpate his religion merely by denying it. He saw the face of God in Nature, but he saw it as the unspeakable Other, and he gauged man against it. The proletarian critics of the thirties, realizing this, denounced him, despising him as a fascist, and they have come to nought. The razzle-dazzle New Critics of the forties attacked him, despising his work as unmitigated flannel-mouthed inflation, and they have come to nought. The fashionable existential critics of the fifties ignored him, despising him as hopelessly simplistic and archaic, and they have come to nought. (I use the figure "come to nought" not in the sense that these movements are valueless, but that their opinions have not proved conclusive. "Nothing," someone has said, "dates more quickly than literary criticism.") Unchastened, Jeffers continued to delineate, in the tremendous vehicle of his verse, the fallen nature of man, its passion, its violence, incest, rapacity, perversity, cunning, compulsiveness and despair, its exaltation and catastrophe. In the primordial images of nature, over against the coagulation that passes for civilization, he saw and affirmed the majestic countenance of the divine, and few of this earth's too-few have ever rendered it so superbly.

And so, inevitably, we arrive at the Final Work.

*

One always awaits the posthumous work of a great writer with apprehension. Has old age perhaps dispersed the powers of youth? Too often the energies that built a magnificent *corpus* are pemitted to grind mechanically on, reproducing the idiom but not the inspiration of the master. Weighing *The Beginning and the End* in the hand, it is pleasant to record that the old fighter made it through.

Not that we are given the awesome spectacle of a Beethoven equalling if not transcending his periods of power; this book is a satisfying *coda* rather than an inimitable Last Quartet. But whatever can be cited against it (and the wearisome list of automatic censures may with equal force be directed against this one) it cannot be said that it is tedious and dull. The idiom is there, surely, but the genius is there also. The marvelous energy remains unabated to the end. If the ideas are only slightly modified with the perspective of old age, the grasp of visual imagery is every bit as sure as it was in the days of his strength, and one is made aware in a strange new way of underlying rhetorical assets that the earlier intensity had tended to conceal. For instance, his ability virtually to shamble through flat statement, yet somehow weave all together into a comprehensive whole, bodying forth the substance of an attitude almost without devices, is remarkable:

> If God has been good enough to give you a poet
> Then listen to him. But for God's sake let him alone until he is dead;
>   no prizes, no ceremony,
> They kill the man. A poet is one who listens
> To nature and his own heart; and if the noise of the world grows up
>   around him, and if he is tough enough,
> He can shake off his enemies but not his friends.
> That is what withered Wordsworth and muffled Tennyson, and
>   would have killed Keats; that is what makes
> Hemingway play the fool and Faulkner forget his art.

There is a distinct contemporaneity in that. And even the modish "crisis of personality" emphasis finds representation, though obviously taken without reference to the current fashionable trend. Nevertheless it touches its terror with an authenticity that many youthful agonizers bent on converting their *angst* into verse, might envy:

> *If you keep command of yourself*
> *You can hear almost anything. But man must rest,*
> *A man must sleep: that is, abandon control: then all the sick demons*
> *Take him in charge. Who ever heard of a pleasant dream?*
> *Fear and remorse are monstrously exaggerated,*
> *And fear of responsibility: that is what drags us*
> *Out of our beds into the bitter black night*
> *To walk the floor and shudder and regain control,*
> *Else we should lie and scream. I seem to hear in the nights*
> *Many estimable people screaming like babies.*
> *I bite my lips and feel my way to the window,*
> *Where the moon rakes through cloud, the wind pants like a dog and*
> *   the ocean*
> *Tears at his shore, gray claws of a great cat*
> *Slitting the granite. The elements thank God are well enough,*
> *It is only man must be always wakeful, steering through hell.*

For one thing the book stands square because there is no minor narrative to deplete the cumulative effect. Instead, we have a book of emphatic shorter poems, the medium which many feel always evidenced Jeffers' greatest strength. Some of these come near to equalling anything he ever wrote for terseness and trenchancy. All of them summon up his inner potential of power, ruggedness, audacity, contemptuous disdain. That disdain is for literary success no less than for material complacency —utterly disdainful of the lost recognition once lavished upon him.

Still, the mood is somehow different, for all the didacticism. It is no longer that of a young man newly disillusioned with the idealism of his febrile youth and forging out a "true" perspec-

tive from the raw stuff of intuition. The mood is rather that of
an old man stubbornly clinging to the opinions of his maturity,
and asserting them over against the capacity of age for transforming opinion into wisdom. (One of the liabilities of age, one
realizes, is this very refusal to accept the potential it inherently
possesses, the potential which it alone offers for transforming
perspective.) At a grosser level you see half-cracked old lumber-
jacks on Skid Row stubbornly clinging to the emblems of their
productive vigor — tin hats, red flannel shirts, even defanged
calk boots — obstinately refusing to concede that life has
brought them any further perspective. This attitude is simply
pride, and it is traceable here, mildly flavoring the old conviction.
It shows itself mostly in the first section, wherein the didactic
poems have been grouped. It is the poorest section, offending
chiefly through the notorious tendentiousness, but still, for all
that, powerfully expressed.

The other sections are better, particularly the one entitled
"Autobiographical," the mood more lyrical, the keen eye whet-
ted to the fine art of direct registration, and personal incidents
told with marvelous delineation. If the sense of wonder and awe
that occasioned the early great breakthrough are gone — that
sense of revealment and almost inexpressible mystery of natural
being that made such poems as "Night," "Continent's End,"
"Hurt Hawks," and so many others, masterpieces of intuitive
expression — yet the energy remains, the undeviating capacity
to say what is meant without equivocation. And that is great
enough for any man to go out on. It might have been dull, fatu-
ous and mediocre. Robinson Jeffers could never be mediocre.
As if to sum up perfectly the implications of his life's whole
magnificent achievement, the last lines of the book deliver it:

However — look again before you go.
The wings and the wild hungers, the wave-worn skerries, the
*   bright quick minnows*
Living in terror to die in torment —
Man's fate and theirs — and the island rocks and immense ocean
*   beyond, and Lobos*
Darkening above the bay: they are beautiful?
That is their quality: not mercy, not mind, not goodness, but the
*   beauty of God.*

5

Hellenistics

A study of the political attitude of Robinson
Jeffers, written to contradict the impression that
he was consciously or unconsciously a
fascist. In passing it takes up also the cases of
such notable twentieth century writers as
D. H. Lawrence, Ezra Pound, T. S. Eliot, and
William Butler Yeats, and tries to throw some light
on the distinction between politics
and literature.

> Be happy, adjust your economics to the new abundance.
> One is neither saint nor devil, to wish
> The intolerable nobler alternative.
> —The Trap

In concluding my analysis of Jeffers' poem "Post Mortem" I spoke of how the poet serves his race: "In the purification ritual which is his act of creation we too can touch something of his search for cleanness, and by gazing with him into the pool of man's self, confront our own hostilities, return to life fortified against them, for ours are his, as his are ours." It is in some such context that I would like to take up the troubling problem of Jeffers' so-called fascism, an epithet first applied to him in the nineteen-thirties. Squires writes:

> Along with the Marxists emerged the "anti-fascists" whose concerns were social without being Marxian and Christian without being religious. Halford E. Luccock, though admitting that he did not feel qualified to thread his way through Jeffers' poetry, still felt qualified to analyze it:
>
> ". . . [He] acclaims the superman, rejects the Christian God, the Christian and humanitarian scale of values. He has incidental criticism of the devastation which the pursuit of money has brought about in life. But when one asks to what Jeffers' glorification of violence leads, the familiar outlines of fascism appear, including faith in a strong man, a "Fuehrer" inhibited by no weakening ethical superstitions. Surely Jeffers is a supreme example of Walter Lippmann's phrase, "trading a majestic faith for a trivial illusion."
>
> Others in the touchy times of the late 1930's found Jeffers, who in *The Women at Point Sur* (1927) argues specifically against the Nietzschean ideals, an exponent of the superman. And they found him the antichrist, while ignoring that he is probably the most deeply religious of all twentieth-century American poets.

Now the taint of fascism is a stigma attached to the names of some of the foremost modern poets. Pound, Yeats and Eliot, all "makers of modern literature," have been able to survive the

crippling effects of this taint. Because they are æsthetically in-
fluential they have retained the right to be considered as artists
despite the censures attached to their political views. With Jeffers
this has not been so. While not the chief stricture, the allegation
of fascism does militate against him as a man and hence as an
artist. Until the matter is clarified it will remain one of the factors precluding acceptance of him as a poet.

Furthermore, in treating of the problem as it applies to
Jeffers, any forthcoming insight may well have a more general
reference. For, though men like Pound and Yeats and Eliot have
survived the ordeal of the passing of fascism, and are secure in
their place, it still surrounds their image, tainting it, and giving
rise to serious misgivings about the nature of their work, and
indeed about the role of the artist in the modern world. In a
significant review of D.H. Lawrence, in the magazine *Ramparts*, Samuel Hynes writes:

> The problem that D. H. Lawrence raises for us is of a kind that many
> of the best writers of his generation pose for our generation. Like
> Pound, like Wyndham Lewis, like Yeats and Eliot to a lesser extent,
> Lawrence believed in, and made his art out of ideas which history
> forbids us to endorse. He was a part of that reactionary swing in the
> first third of this century that paradoxically produced a literary rev-
> olution, of which we are all the beneficiaries. But the movement also
> fostered social and political results which are less admirable, and we
> have inherited those ills, too. And so, while Lawrence could talk,
> with apparent confidence, about "dark fructifying powers," and the
> wisdom of the blood, we, forty years later, have seen what fruit
> those dark powers bore, and must, if we are rational, reject the idea
> that man can trust those forces in his nature which mind does not
> control . . .

In engaging this problem Hynes raises one possible solution, a
tempting one, and in fact the common one adopted by critics
when forced to deal with the baffling problem of the contradiction in all these men between literary performance and political belief.

We might solve the problem, I suppose, by postulating *two* Lawrences: Lawrence-the-Maker, a poetic, if somewhat neurotic artist, marvelously responsive to sensory experience, and good on nature and emotional states; and Lawrence-the-Judge, at his mildest a critic of the evils of industrial society, at his worst a messiah-manqué.

But he has no sooner posited this solution than he is forced to reject it, for

it avoids the central, sticky point — that both Lawrences are the same man, and that both are present in the best of his work . . . We can't simply lay the two Lawrences end to end; they insist on being judged together . . . at the end of his career, as at the beginning, Lawrence was both Maker and Judge, concerned at once with the transcription of intense experience and with criticism of the modern world.

Consequently, we must include in our judgments of Lawrence both an awareness of his achievements as an artist and a recognition of his inadequacies as a thinker. In his casual writing — his letters, his psychological books, and the worst of his novels and stories — Lawrence the Judge is likely to dominate, and when that happens he is clearly in the stream of an ugly twentieth-century movement — the anti-intellectual, authoritarian, "blood-knowledge" strain that ended in Nazism. But in his best work he demonstrates — as Yeats and Eliot also demonstrate — that the true artist inevitably complicates and qualifies his most extreme ideas when he turns them into art.

Yet Hynes, despite his own realizations, does not quite escape the temptation to play upon the dichotomy between Lawrence-the-Judge as an inferior artist, and Lawrence-the-Maker as a superior one, no doubt because a certain shrillness of tone in Lawrence's polemics encourages this recourse. But others under the cloud are harder to deal with. The poet Donald Davie writing recently in *The Manchester Guardian* attacks Yeats for fascism, which he claims to be fully documented in Yeats's record as an Irish Senator. Centering in on Pound's praise of Yeats's last poems as proof, he asks:

To be blunt, isn't "Under Ben Bulben" just the poem we should expect to be applauded by a rabid Fascist such as Pound then was? Isn't
the fascism there in the style, as well as in the blood-boltered content ("Send war in our time, O Lord!")? And isn't it the fascism, in
part, that makes one of Yeats's rhetorics unacceptable to poets
today?

This charge of the possibility of a fascist style, a fascist rhetoric,
is one we will consider later. Returning to Hynes's solution to
the situation of Lawrence we find:

> The problem that Lawrence saw — the problem of individual self-
> fulfillment in a dehumanizing modern world—is real, and brilliantly
> realized in the best novels. It was only when he turned to answers
> that he became shrill, irrational, and unhealthy. Perhaps the lesson
> is that, for our time, the art is in the problems, not in the answers.
> Or perhaps that has always been the artist's answer to experience.

All this, of course, might be said with equal cogency of Jeffers.
If it serves for Lawrence and Pound and Eliot and Yeats, then it
will serve for the Californian too. It is not a matter of the intelligence. If Eliot indicted Lawrence "for what we ordinarily call
thinking" what does it prove about Eliot's brains since he is
painted with the same brush? Who today will defend Eliot for
having "better" reasons for inclining to fascism than Lawrence
had? But from the point of view of furthering the cause of Jeffers, one could simply point to the dilemma raised in the case of
the others, men accepted in the highest echelons of art and
achievement today, and simply leave it at that.

But it is not my intention to leave it at that. To accord the
artist, as Hynes does, the right to ask questions, but to deny to
him, as Hynes does, the right to answer them, is unrealistic. If
you are going to honor the artist, and profit by his questions,
then you are going to have to come to terms with his answers.
You may not like what they are, but you must consider them,
and acknowledge that in some way they are at one with the

questions proposed. It may well be that simply considering them will reveal the real reasons for their existence, why they were asked at all. Because critics are critics rather than poets they often do not *feel* the problems as the poet experienced them, and hence have no real grasp of the kinds of solutions he is proposing. If we assume that the problem of the poet is simply the problem of an industrial society, then his answer indeed becomes absurd. I think all these poets would defend themselves by saying that if we like the question but do not like the answer, then we never understood the question at all. I confess this in myself. I acknowledge that I must, therefore, look more deeply into the question proposed.

II

Fascism is an attempt to forge a bond between an historic sacral culture with its roots in the past, and an emergent pluralist mentality not yet thoroughly formalized in a living tradition. A sacral culture is one integrated around a limited cosmology, made permeable by religious belief and religious practices, and generally codified in dogma. When human initiative expands its fields of knowledge and challenges the ancient cosmology, latent ingredients in the dominant society begin to emerge. Because they are potential they are projected into the future, schematized philosophically, and in time become codified in law: human betterment based not on traditional patterns but upon philosophical abstraction, the liberal syndrome.

If the cosmological shift has been profound, as was the shift from a Ptolemaic to a Copernican cosmology, and as is the shift from a Newtonian to an Einsteinian one, then the integrity of the old sacral hegemony is threatened, and the tension between the ancient and secure Establishment and the developing Movement becomes acute. As the culture shifts from sacral to pluralist norms it progresses through a series of revolutionary crises, each exacting from the social body various degrees of resistance and participation. In these the artists, the poets, take no small part. They either project into the future a utopian visionary hope, or they concretize upon the past an equally visionary mythical mystique. In the Romantic movement which opened the nineteenth century it was the former. In the industrial crisis of the third decade of this one it was, among the poets we have mentioned, the latter. For, if civil or international war, or particularly the introduction of new inventions, accelerate the pace of the Movement beyond the capacity of the society to adjust to it, then the social fabric becomes threatened, and remedies are introduced to bridge the developing gap, or accomplish the breakover into a totally new phase. The third decade of this century, across which the quasi-fascist writers retained their prestige and their æsthetic domination, was a period characterized by an ancient sacral culture in the last throes of transformation between the wide-open pluralistic society projected by *laissez faire* capitalism, and the accelerated version of a utopian finality proposed by bolshevist communism. If such poets were reactionary it was because they saw, to a man, values in the old sacral orientation which were being jettisoned, with totally inadequate substitutes offered in their place.

The bolshevist triumph in Russia during the First World War had been so sudden and so total that it stunned Europe. Professing to be sacrally liberated, in fact it implemented the residual sacral elements in the culture by utopianism, projecting them into the future. The writers of whom we are speaking saw that this transfer was a delusion. Their attempt was to formalize those sacral values in their art, in a conscious endeavor to contain them against that threatening eventuality, so that a more realizable future might be secured. Whether they saw this in terms of a return to a pre-capitalistic fiscal policy as did Pound; whether they saw it in terms of retention of hierarchical aristocracy as did Eliot and Yeats; whether they saw it in terms of a preservation of instinctual life as did Lawrence; whether they saw it pantheistically as the essential bond between the individual consciousness and the cosmos, as did Jeffers; each was concerned with the retention of subsistent sacral values as the key to the wholeness of man — a wholeness which the triumph of humanistic atheism, with its establishment in industrial society, had threatened, and which bolshevist revolution hoped to make permanent by preempting the future.

Each of these men, ironically enough, save Jeffers alone, lived to see his vision appropriated by some political movement of the time and debased through aggrandizement and chicanery. Pound identified himself with an existent fascist state and lived to see it smashed. Eliot and Yeats saw their vision of an aristocracy travestied in the imposed class structures of Mussolini and Franco. Lawrence saw intuition into man's need for orgiastic renewal appallingly appropriated by Hitlerian primitivism. Jeffers alone lived to see his version of man's salvation ignored by any political aggrandizement, because, as he well knew, it was not capable of political formulation. But that the appropriation of a poet's vision into political categories does not jeopardize the cruciality of his questions, even a writer like Hynes allows.

Whether or not these political appropriations truly constitute the "answers" of such men is a matter open to debate, and not germane here. What is germane is that their own answers were of a piece with their questions, and their questions are definable only in terms of the answers proposed. All of them saw that the projective pluralistic elements in the society had swept far beyond the sacral roots, and all of them attempted to re-establish, through the chief means available to them (their art) those values in society. It is no good saying, as Hynes does, that "while Lawrence could talk, with apparent confidence, about 'dark fructifying powers,' and the wisdom of the blood, we, forty years later, have seen what fruit those dark powers bore, and must, if we are rational, reject the idea that man can trust those forces in his nature which mind does not control." What he does not see is that Lawrence's answer lies in his art. Because of his simplistic equation between art and politics Hynes cuts himself off from the source of all Lawrence is offering him.

> It is surprising that Lawrence's life-affirming ideas of love and freedom and self-fulfillment could turn so readily into power and authority and self-abnegation. These three repulsive books—*Aaron's Rod, Kangaroo,* and *The Plumed Serpent*—are all in a sense political novels, though it might be more precise to call them messianic fantasies; in them the will-to-love is succeeded by the will-to-power (and its necessary correlative, the will to submit to the power of a leader). I don't see how any of them can be read in our time without horror and revulsion.

If Mr. Hynes shuts himself off from the archetypal sources in Lawrence's vision by virtue of his revulsion from their social consequences when attempted politically in our time, he is nullifying Lawrence's function as a true agent of those forces for our time. If this is tantamount to saying that fascism was an æsthetic movement mistakenly applied to politics, then let it stand. Whatever you choose to call it, the only way that the sacral truth inherent in aristocracy, or orgiastic primitivism, or cosmological pantheism, can be realistically retained today is in the æsthetic domain. If Hitler made the colossal mistake of trying to apply the visionary worlds of Wagner and Nietzsche to concrete politics, that was tragic indeed. But only less tragic is the mistake of Hynes who is revulsed from æsthetic sources because those sources were misapplied. For if the critic, the evaluative intellectual, teeters toward this very error in reverse form, how can we be surprised when the obsessed politician joyfully embraces it?

III

What we have been saying, then, is that æsthetic movements and political movements arise out of the same underlying archetypal needs, are different forms of the same psychic manifestation. These needs are truths. If they are not soluble in terms of political realities, all the more crucial must be their efficacy in æsthetic ones. Not only is it erroneous of Davie to repudiate a magnificent poem like "Under Ben Bulben" because its very style, its very rhetoric are thought to be "fascist," it is downright dangerous for him to do so. For it means that preconceptual archetypal realities upon which such works have their relevance remain unstemmed, and psychological investigation has assured us that such evasion is fatal. Like the politically oriented idealist who, arising from sleep, represses a terrible dream because the violence he commits in it is plainly "fascistic," he ends up, comes the crisis, performing in the name of necessity the violence he abhors. If Hynes, remembering the concentration camps of the immediate past, cannot muster enough æsthetic sophistication to read *The Plumed Serpent* without revulsion, then he is merely contributing to the concentration camps of the future, for he is making the same æsthetic mistake as Goebbels.

One function of the poet is to project the possible. The social philosopher does the same thing in terms of ideational social norms. Both work with the creative intuition, which, playing upon the experience of the past, projects their relevance in terms of new applications or future extensions. The poet, in this regard, differs from the philosopher by operating in the domain of the feelings. The imaginative correlative of his emotion-state, his feeling-state, is registered in what may be called his mood. By registration of his mood in the concretization of æsthetic form he bodies forth, makes realizable, the content of the vision of the possible which he experiences. It is

this that permits us to assent or dissent in a way not possible
with the social philosopher. At a higher level he makes his
vision permanent by virtue of its inherent æsthetic, which protects it from misapplication in the phenomenal world, because
once it is translated into another idiom it vanishes. When Yeats
writes:

> You that Mitchel's prayer have heard,
> 'Send war in our time, O Lord!'
> Know that when all words are said
> And a man is fighting mad,
> Something drops from eyes long blind,
> He completes his partial mind,
> For an instant stands at ease,
> Laughs aloud, his heart at peace.
> Even the wisest man grows tense
> With some sort of violence
> Before he can accomplish fate,
> Know his work or choose his mate

he is stating a profound human truth, which no denigration
can impugn, even if it could be proved that Yeats wrote the
words in support of some political movement which we might
abhor. For he is rendering available to the consciousness the
very violence he is predicating, and instituting its uses into
the collective consciousness, freed of the impending consequences its denotative application in his immediate circum-
stances might have occasioned. His poem was born of its time,
but whatever the time that gave it birth, it remains available for
all time to come.

On the other side of the barricade may be cited the poetry of
Mayakovsky, whose "free verse," according to Selden Rodman,
"sparkles with genuine revolutionary élan and ironic wit and is
said to be as popular with millions of Russians today as when he
declaimed it like a troubadour of the Middle Ages to mass meetings in the factories of Moscow," words which make me regret

that I do not read Russian. For if the memory of the Stalinist purges which terminated that revolutionary fervor made my disgust of Mayakovsky so profound that I was unable to read him, then I would be in as sorry a position as Mr. Hynes, whose memory of Nazi Youth Rallies isolates him from Lawrence's revivatory approximations.

With these observations we are now able to take up the special case of Jeffers, and discuss some of the elements by which he serves the race in terms of his own attempts at sacral recovery, as man has known it in the past, and his need of it in the future.

IV

It was in the mid-nineteen-thirties that Jeffers began to write the poetry that has compromised his name ever since. It constitutes a substantial body of work, and it cannot be discounted as a passing psychological aberration. Indeed, the mood of that time was so universal and so oppressive that every poet dealing in large and comprehensive themes was forced to take cognizance of it. So powerful was this oppression upon the psyche of the individual poets that it beclouded the interior process and gave rise to a prevalent shrillness and thinness destructive to the deepest æsthetic values, and seriously compromised the function of the poet. When the drift culminated in open warfare in the forties that psychological intensity, in the case of Jeffers, who differed from this solution, became so intense, that some of his most loyal advocates have regretted the work he produced at this time, and have not been slow to indict him for it, in the hope of rescuing from oblivion the greater work that preceded it. Frederic Carpenter, for instance, traces the processive deterioration evidenced by a comparison of his three poems "Shine, Perishing Republic" (1923), "Shine, Republic" (1935), and "Shine, Empire" (1944).

I myself, remembering the appalling pressures of those years, do not indict him. Actually the slackening of tension in certain political poems does not indicate a debility of total creative energy. The "Shine, Empire" of 1944 is no worse than some of the companion pieces of "Shine, Perishing Republic" of 1923, while certain poems in his final volume will take their place in the corpus of his permanent achievement. The psychological balance between involvement and detachment that makes the mind of such a writer is so delicate that any emphatic shift in the collective atmosphere is bound to have its effect. A strong case can be made for his not having spoken until he could speak with detachment; that he was not able to stems doubtless from the same need that made him adopt detachment in the first place: a tremendous concern. In any case, æsthetic lapses in the creative life, like moral lapses in the social one, are indemnified (that is to say, become efficacious for the good) by the conviction with which they are committed. The dedication and thoroughness of the Nazis has torn the mask off conventional anti-Semitism forever. "Shine, Empire" may not have the granitic aloofness we admire in the best Jeffers work, but that it is biting political commentary, that its thesis is at least tenable, and that it has its own lonely eloquence, cannot be denied. Such is its conviction that the very pathos of its comparative weakness makes its point more telling.

V

So much for the general problem. More specifically, I want to consider chiefly one poem, which will stand well enough for Jeffers' work of this period. It is called "Hellenistics," and has the advantage of concretizing all the "fascistic" elements into a single whole. It is also unique in that it evokes an appeal to the same orgiastic sources that motivated Lawrence, sources which the cold-natured Jeffers usually purported to disdain.

Since the orgiastic element of fascism is as repulsive to the contemporary intellectual as its political tyranny, and since this element is convenient to him in distinguishing it from its rival ideology, communism, to meet its problems here will serve for large areas of related issues.

Before taking it up, one thing ought to be settled at the outset, and that is this: it seems obvious that as far as projecting any "actual solutions" goes, the charge attributable to Lawrence can in no wise be levelled against Jeffers. The real solutions of Jeffers seem, on examination, and considered solely from a political standpoint, hardly more dangerous than a kind of frosty isolationism :

> *I too*
> *Believe that the life of men who ride horses, herders of cattle on the*
> *mountain pasture, plowers of remote*
> *Rock-narrowed farms in poverty and freedom, is a good life. At the*
> *far end of those loops of road*
> *Is what will come and destroy it, a rich and vulgar and bewildered*
> *civilization dying at the core . . .*

G. K. Chesterton, an English Catholic of the back-to-the-land movement following the first World War, made the same point :

> To this day the comparatively simple agricultural communities are by far the purest democracies. Democracy is a thing which is always breaking down through the complexity of civilization. Anyone who likes may state it by saying that democracy is the foe of civilization. But he must remember that some of us really prefer democracy to civilization, in the sense of preferring democracy to complexity.

The socialist sweeps these sentiments aside as sheer irrelevancies. Mass society is here; the problems of civilization must be coped with, not shucked; only the committed intellectual can ensure that the truths of man's freedom be preserved in the solution of the problems of production and distribution. If civilization is rich and vulgar and bewildered it is because men of the mind like Jeffers have withdrawn the force of intellect from it and left it in the hands of egomaniacs, aggressive belligerents, and entrepreneurs.

That Jeffers had not withdrawn the force of intellect from it but rather gave that intellect to its critique, however, is the chief cause of the charge of fascism against him. The nature of his critique, which is that of the uninvolved observer upon some lonely mountain top, may be fairly instanced by the poem "Rearmament," published in 1937.

> These grand and fatal movements toward death; the grandeur of
>   the mass
> Makes pity a fool, the tearing pity
> For the atoms of the mass, the persons, the victims, makes it seem
>   monstrous
> To admire the tragic beauty they build.
> It is beautiful as a river flowing or a slowly gathering
> Glacier on a high mountain rock-face,
> Bound to plow down a forest, or as frost in November,
> The gold and flaming death-dance for leaves,
> Or a girl in the night of her spent maidenhood, bleeding and kissing.
> I would burn my right hand in a slow fire
> To change the future . . . I should do foolishly. The beauty of modern
> Man is not in the persons, but in the
> Disastrous rhythms, the heavy and mobile masses, the dance of the
> Dream-led masses down the dark mountain.

It is a beautiful poem, its movement catching up and in fact ennobling the massive destructive forces it memorializes. And it serves us well as an approach to our subject-poem, "Hellenistics," for its final line is not merely a literary metaphor; it is a concrete reference to the Dionysian rites as they were practiced in archaic Greece. Jeffers himself had treated them in "The Humanist's Tragedy," his version of the incident from Euripides' *Bacchæ* where Agave among the maddened dancers dismembers her own son, King Pentheus. Thus what he nailed his thought home with was no idle fancy. Jeffers was seeing through to those involuntary hysterias that sweep through collective movements, and which the Marxist intellectuals of the thirties so feared as the tools by which fascistic autocrats could sway the masses, and were themselves embarrassed by because they had no real defense against the identical charges of abstainers like Jeffers, who persisted in seeing communism and fascism as the two sides of one false coin: the mass compulsions that underswept all the ideologies. Jeffers' reference to the "dream-led masses" takes the source of modern collectivist movements clear back to Mount Cithæron.

E. R. Dodds, in his appendix on Mænadism in *The Greeks and the Irrational*, writes:

> In many societies, perhaps in all societies, there are people for whom, as Mr. Aldous Huxley puts it,"ritual dances provide a religious experience that seems more satisfying and convincing than any other . . . It is with their muscles that they most easily obtain knowledge of the divine." Mr. Huxley thinks that Christianity made a mistake when it allowed the dance to become completely secularized, since, in the words of a Mohammedan sage,"he that knows the Power of the Dance dwells in God."

> But the Power of the Dance is a dangerous power. Like other forms of self-surrender, it is easier to begin than to stop. In the extraordinary dancing madness which periodically invaded Europe from the fourteenth to the seventeenth century, people danced until they dropped — like the dancer at *Bacchæ* 136 or the dancer on a Berlin vase, no. 2471 — and lay unconscious, trodden underfoot by their fellows.

> Also the thing is highly infectious. As Pentheus observes at *Bacchæ* 778, it spreads like wildfire. The will to dance takes possession of people without the consent of the conscious mind: e.g., at Liége in 1374, after certain possessed folk had come dancing half-naked into the town with garlands on their heads, dancing in the name of St. John, we are told that "many persons seemingly sound in mind and body were suddenly possessed by the devils and joined the

dancers"; these persons left house and home, like the Theban women
in the play; even young girls cut themselves off from their family
and friends and wandered away with the dancers.

Jeffers' indiscriminate attribution of these tendencies to the
collective movements of his time disconcerted and then disgust-
ed his fellow intellectuals. The world was in the grip of a
terrible depression that obviously had its roots in *laissez faire*
capitalism, and some sort of collective norm for the regulariza-
tion of the economy was imperative. Instead, the world was
drifting toward war. Intellectuals felt that if they could stop
fascism in Spain and secure the conversion of America to communism the threat of war could be averted, since the doctrinaire
marxist thesis had it that capitalist economies (and their off-
spring, fascist ones) of necessity had recourse to violence to
sustain their existence. Had Jeffers at that moment contented
himself with applying his strictures to capitalist and fascist
nations alone, he could have enjoyed immense prestige. Instead
he persisted in looking through to the unconscious components
behind the mass movements as a whole, which for him proved
an indictment of all collective solutions, even though he acknowledged the incidental salubrity of some side effects. For
this salubrity has been long known. Dodds continues:

> in Greece the ritual oreibasia at a fixed date may originally have
> developed out of spontaneous attacks of mass hysteria. By canalizing
> such hysteria in an organized rite once in two years, the Dionysiac
> cult kept it within bounds and gave it a relatively harmless outlet.
> What the παροσος of the *Bacchæ* depicts is hysteria subdued to the
> service of religion; what happened on Mount Cithæron was hysteria
> in the raw, the dangerous Bacchism which descends as a punishment
> on the too respectable and sweeps them away against their will.
> Dionysus is present in both: like St. John or St. Vitus, he is the cause
> of madness and the liberator from madness, βακχος and Λγσιος. We
> must keep this ambivalence in mind if we are rightly to understand
> the play. To resist Dionysus is to repress the elemental in one's own

nature; the punishment is the sudden complete collapse of the in-
ward dykes when the elemental breaks through perforce and civilization vanishes.

That Jeffers was not unaware of the salubrious aspects of the
collectivities will be seen in his poem "Hellenistics," but it is
hardly surprising that his fellow writers of the period, who
justified their own participation on the basis of proletarian-
intellectual classlessness, were not edified. To them, caught
up as they were with the overriding necessity of stopping the
spread of fascism in Spain and of war in the world, counting all
on the ability of the democracies to contain that threat before
the universal carnage burst upon mankind, everything he was
saying seemed like social and intellectual bankruptcy.

If today we have more detachment, we still are unforgiving,
too stung yet with the rigors of those old hardships. To admire
such a poem merely because it is massive and beautiful, when
its consequences were so problematical and sheer, seems perverse. "I don't see how any of them can be read in our time
without revulsion." To say you would cut your hand off to
change the future, but not lift that hand in its defense, is cheap
fatalism, and unworthy of the American ethos. The intellectual
who survived the times, determined to remain true to the best
he ever believed, in a world of conflicting ideologies and unpre-
dictable fortunes, can still read Mayakovsky's poems for their
"revolutionary *elan*" and "ironic wit," and hence recapture the
relish of the camaraderie of those years, but this ponderous
Jeffersian pessimism continues to leave him unpleasantly cold.
Is it beautiful? Yes, perhaps, in small doses, that will be con-
ceded — has never, in fact, really been denied. But he will insist
that the beauty is life-destructive and irrelevant and dangerous.
It is the very existence of such a poem which keeps him unconvinced when shown a dozen others specifically denying the
"solution" of fascism —"The Coast Road," for instance, from

which we have quoted. For to admire the "beauty" of modern war *is* fascism. He remembers Mussolini's son, an airman, describing the impression of blossoming bombs as he drops them on the mud huts of Ethiopia, and he curses D'Annunzio for placing such ideas in the minds of youth. He curses Jeffers. If his feeling is understandable, he ought at least to realize that in cherishing it he is committing the first intellectual sin: the failure to distinguish.

VI

But the poem I have chosen to consder more closely is not so typical, nor so detached, and therefore is more problematical. After all, a poet-prophet on a mountain top is only irritating. In "Hellenistics" Jeffers moves up closer in involvement, and begins to activate within himself some of those archetypal forces which were governing the rise of fascism in the world at that time, containing them and disdainful of them as he begins, and as he proceeds, but releasing them and valorizing them in his conclusion. Whether or not in valorizing them he also drenches them sufficiently in the æsthetic, in the universal, to render them immune to political appropriation, will depend upon his genius as a poet, his powers of formulation, and his intrinsic purity of heart.

The poem originates as a somber meditation on the Greek ideal at a time of great social stress, potential of war. Remember the year is 1937, the Chamberlain era. The democracies in the West are paralyzed with fear before the threats of the totalitarians. The nations have not yet recovered from the Great Depression, whose apathy still pervades them. They are paralyzed with guilt for their vengefulness at Versailles, and the vast whoopee party of the twenties. The hangover, the depression, has not yet been lifted. As we saw elsewhere the dominant poets were seeking a recovery of the active principle, seeking

their roots back in the fundamental reserves of man's traditional nature. Yeats, remember, is writing: "Even the wisest man
grows tense/With some sort of violence." Tense with violence,
groping down within himself for its meaning and its clue, Jeffers begins. As we listen we remember that he read Greek at
the age of five, that in Europe his tutors called him "the little
Spartan." The first part of the poem is as follows:

> I look at the Greek-derived design that nourished my infancy — this
> Wedgwood copy of the Portland vase:
> Someone had given it to my father — my eyes at five years old used
> to devour it by the hour.
>
> I look at a Greek coin, four-drachma piece struck by Lysimachus:
> young Alexander's head
> With the horns of Ammon and brave brow-ridges, the bright pride
> and immortal youth and wild sensitiveness.
>
> I think of Achilles, Sappho, the Nike. I think of those mercenaries
> who marched in the heart of Asia
> And lived to salute the sea: the lean faces like lance-heads, the grace
> of panthers. The dull welter of Asia.
>
> I am past childhood, I look at this ocean and the fishing birds, the
> streaming skerries, the shining water,
> The foam-heads, the exultant dawn-light going west, the pelicans,
> their huge wings half folded, plunging like stones.
>
> Whatever it is catches my heart in its hands, whatever it is makes
> me shudder with love
> And painful joy and the tears prickle . . . the Greeks were not its
> inventors. The Greeks were not the inventors
>
> Of shining clarity and jewel-sharp form and the beauty of God. He
> was free with men before the Greeks came:
> He is here naked on the shining water. Every eye that has a man's
> nerves behind it has known him.

We are back at a familiar Jeffersian concept, the identity
between beauty and divinity. And the prescription of his infan-
cy is important, indicating that both an identity and a progression, begun in the contemplation of the finest period of the

human past, has been increased and concentrated, rather than debilitated and stultified, in the images of nature before his eyes. For him, growing up means the growing out of the matrix of man's cultural presuppositions. At any rate, Greece might have been the quintessence of human achievement, but could not obviate the universality of human ignorance:

> I think of the dull welter of Asia. I think of squalid savages along
>   the Congo: the natural
> Condition of man, that makes one say of all beasts "They are not
>   contemptible. Man is contemptible." I see
>
> The squalor of our own frost-bitten forefathers. I will praise the
>   Greeks for having pared down the shame of three vices
> Natural to man and no other animal, cruelty and filth and supersti-
>   tion, grained in man's making.

Whitman has said it in another way: "I think I could turn and live with animals . . . they do not sweat and whine about their condition . . .they do not lie awake in the dark and weep for their sins." But Jeffers' comment is simply in passing, his mood is not that of Whitman's liberation, but of the hopelessness of human enlightenment. Xenophon who marched eastward had given him, in his mind's eye, the clue to that situation, the Greek clarity in the Asiatic mass. And all the religious superstitions, Moses, Christ, Mohammed, riverbound Egypt and "holy paralytic India," the long bondage of man's adhesion of self-projection. It is too much for him. He opens up on the cruciality of the poem and its implication focuses.

> The age darkens, Europe mixes her cups of death, all the little
>   Cæsars fidget on their thrones,
> The old wound opens its clotted mouth to ask for new wounds.

Of these lines William Van Wyck commented at the time of their publication: "The function of the poet is to say greatly in a few miraculously chosen words, the epitome of things. Pages and pages of thought could not set down more wisely or more exactly the facts." In the Europe of 1937 this was indeed the way it was. But Jeffers continues:

> *Men will fight through; men have tough hearts.*
> *Men will fight through to the autumn flowering and ordered*
> *prosperity.*

He too is forced to acknowledge the tremendous emphasis of the time on utopianism. It is as if the awful longing of his compatriots for that realization, which technology had for the first time made available to the race, was opened to him, and he too acknowledges it, he cannot deny its tremendous appeal and hope.

> *They will lift their heads in the great cities*
> *Of the empire and say: Freedom? Freedom was a fire. We*
> *are well quit of freedom, we have found prosperity."*

But it is his irony that gives the game away. The salutation to the toughness of man's heart and the tenacity of his striving is mocked by the vision of that end, a utopia in which freedom (man's most prized possession and the thing that distinguishes him from the animals, though its misuse makes him contemptible), this freedom, this prize, is being thrown away again for "an ordered prosperity."

They will say, "Where now are the evil prophets?" meaning of course himself and other nay sayers who denied the communal dream and predicted disaster. So he acknowledges the attainability of the utopian goal; he concedes it, but is not convinced.

> *Thus for a time*
> *in the age's afterglow, the sterile time;*
> *But the wounds drain, and freedom has died, slowly the machines*
> *break down, slowly the wilderness returns.*

In his inveterate consciousness he knows that freedom is the one essential that man possesses, and that when man denies his freedom for security he denies his nature. His security cannot survive.

Then he breaks forth in the great pæan to the future. He projects so far ahead that it takes on a kind of mythical universality to match the mythical character of the Greek past upon which he had founded his vision. It is a very strange passage, and is not immediately consistent, although the poem is not conceived in a difficult mode. But there is a shift forward in mood, in inner psychic polarities, which constitutes the real emotional center of the poem. I have spoken in earlier parts of this essay of how the "reactionary" poets tried to project or retain psychic elements of the race's sacral past. He has just given us the utopian vision and the cost at which it is purchased; security in exchange for freedom, and his irony has proclaimed, through his diction, that as far as he is concerned the future can have it; it is not worth the price it is bought with.

But in this last section of the poem all that seems to drop away, and as if some psychic referent from the mass needs of his time, the despised sources of collective human nature that had produced the "dull welter of Asia," emerges. (Or can it be the Greek Dionysian rites to which he has reference?) It is as if he sees the root behind these modern movements, sensing it in the Nazi Youth Rallies and the monumental mass meetings in Red Square, seeing it and acknowledging its truth, as he despises its jeopardy of essential human freedom, the core of individuality and personality sacrificed to projective superstitions—even so his coldness and detachment and contempt yield at last, and he turns and makes his acknowledgement, his concession to collective energy and force, with its blind forbidden ending, and its impossible conditions.

> Oh distant future children going down to the foot of the mountain,
>   the new barbarism, the night of time,
> Mourn your own dead if you remember them, but not for civilization,
>   not for our scuttled futilities.
> You are saved from being little entrails feeding large brains, you are

saved from being little empty bundles of enjoyment,
You are not to be fractional supported people but complete men; you
will guard your own heads, you will have proud eyes.

And suddenly there breaks out of him a celebration to the
orgiastic source of all religion and all poetry, a celebration to
danger and awe, to power, transcendence, purposiveness, consummation — the deep motivational element of the psyche
which underlies the roots of participation and in its blindness is
so patently corruptible to base expediency, but in spite of which,
in every age, retains its essentially sacral character, its religious
origin.

You will stand among the spears when you meet; life will be lovely
and terrible again, great and in earnest;
You will know hardship, hunger and violence: these are not the
evils: what power can save you from the real evils

Of barbarism? What poet will be born to tell you to hate cruelty and
filth? What prophet will warn you
When the witch-doctors begin dancing, or if any man says "I am a
priest," to kill them with spears?

The fist pounds the poem to a close. There is no gainsaying the
power, imprecational, austere, menacing, righteousness adum-
brating itself in the strophes of finality. Obviously the poet is
purging the orgiastic sources of the future against the institutional sinecures that disfigured its past, seeking to liberate it
from doctrine entirely, as if such doctrinization itself were the
real barbarism, and in this we may in fact be glimpsing his
residual Protestantism. In the beginning of his poem, contem-
plating the evocative Greek objects, he had rejected any such
thing as a repository of truth. "The Greeks were not the inven-
tors of crystal form . . . He is here *naked* on the shining water."
So he gives the future its spears and its loveliness, because they
are positive, direct, unequivocal, the cleanliest symbols of volition and realization.

But it cannot be denied that the appeal to the blood, as we

commonly identify it with fascism, is here in play: the violence of the spears, the primitivism of the movement, the exultance in physical association and the intoxication of corporate impetus. So too is the imprecation to violence. Life is to be lovely and terrible again, that sense of the consequentiality we saw in "Rearmament" where he conjoined violence and sexuality, "a girl in the night of her spent maidenhood, bleeding and kissing." Love and violence, and the powerful substratum of this imprecation. Earlier, in his poem "At the Fall of an Age," which narrates the death of Helen of Troy, he had lined the Myrmidons up in just such a file as here projected. They had been commissioned to follow Helen so that no man could possess her after Achilles, but they were not to prevent her death, and as she is captured and hanged they look on, between the spears, chanting:

> Look under the torches, Oh King, that flare in the wind of night,
> Look under the torches.
> No Dorians are we; they planted strange seed in Asia who buried
>   Achilles,
> Power to pierce death, helmeted heads cracking the grass-roots,
> Power to be born again.
> Come down and behold us Oh King of heaven and Oh hawks
>   of Caucasus
> Come down and behold us,
> You African lions in the tawny wilderness roar in the storm,
> For our master is joined with the beauty he remembered in death,
>   with the splendor of the earth,
> While the King of Laconia howls like a starved dog
> In the rain, in the violent lightnings, in the gaps of night, and we
>   hold the gates.

This is orgiastic enough, certainly, but it is a reconstitution of past legendary sources and as such has an unquestionable æsthetic legitimacy. But in "Hellenistics" he is not asking us to consider the past, he is inviting us (is he not?) to seize the future and, like all fascism, to seize it in bloodshed and violence!

And what if he is? At whom, pray, is his violence directed? The priest, yes, the priest. Those with long memories know that at the time he is writing, in 1937, among intellectuals, the image of the priest is indeed little more than that of witch doctor . In Catholic Italy were not the priests blessing Mussolini's troops as they embarked for Abyssinia? In Catholic Spain were they not blessing Franco's armies as they crushed Guernica? Even in Germany were not the Roman Catholic bishops urging their cohorts to support Hitler's armies? Thou hast said well, Jeffers. Priestcraft *is* fascism. And priestcraft and fascism must be crushed together. It is good that in communist Russia, the true anti-fascist citadel in a Europe on the verge of madness, your words are verified now in the present, rather than in the past or the future.

> *What prophet will warn you*
> *When the witch-doctors begin dancing, or if any man says "I am a*
> *priest," to kill them with spears?*

In lieu of spears machine guns will serve. One can almost hear the Abraham Lincoln Brigadiers chanting these sentiments, if not the strophes, as they burn the Spanish churches.

But hold. This poem is anti-priest. If priesthood is fascism, if fascism sustains itself behind the surplice of the priest, how, then, can this be a fascist poem?

It is very bewildering. Political poetry always is, is it not? The political poet, if he be true poet, is always uncovering more than his slogans intended. No sooner does he start to chant than he finds himself down in the ancient pre-political psychic levels, where the elemental images emerge, where the powerful trans-rational values, so profound, religious and meaningful, begin to germinate. No sooner does he arrive at the political rally when, chanting his poems, he finds men gripped by motivations that antedate the whole structure of economic society, that tap at substrata more eternal and more basic than all the currents of his thought.

He ought not be surprised. I, the priest-killer, could tell him.

For consider. I am a Catholic. On every Good Friday, along with every other Catholic, along with every other Christian, I slay the supreme Priest, Christ Jesus, King and Redeemer of men. I, the eternal centurion, open His side with the insatiable lance, symbol of volition and execution, and verify His blood, symbol of loveliness and realization.

More. Before I can do this He has already done it Himself. Every day on the altar I behold it. He, the supreme Priest, Christ Jesus, lays down His life in sacrifice, pours out His blood for my wine, His flesh for my bread. In His archetypal death and dismemberment a ravenous hunger gorges on finality, the cannibalistic heart of man is fed over and over on the substance of its obsession: the flesh of God.

Actually, Jeffers knew this. He himself once put in the mouth of Jesus the underlying salience of His terrible immolation:

> Only a crucified
> God can fill the wolf bowels of Rome; only a torture
> high up in the air, and crossed beams, hang sovereign
> When the blond savages exalt their kings; when the
> north moves, and the hairy-breasted north is unbound,
> And Cæsar a mouse under the hooves of the horses ...

If you are going to redeem mankind, the whole of mankind (and why sacrifice for less?), then the most archaic needs, the fundamental stupor, must be grappled and taken up. If Jeffers the philosopher, the mind of the man, attacked religion, Jeffers the poet, in his archaic images, reconstituted it as he spoke. Among the spears and the loveliness he was immolating his intelligence to his heart. The archetypal reconstitution, given up blindly out of the orgiastic center of the soul, is the eternal truth, manifested over and over. The artist can never escape it; once he places himself in the creative dimension the primordial symbols emerge. *In the depths of his imagery the poet cannot lie!* Neither could Jeffers. Neither could Eliot the Aristocrat. Neither could Pound the Propagandist. Neither could Yeats the Yea-sayer. Lawrence's dark gods are calling indeed, but what they are calling is neither old nor new. It is eternal. It exists in the mouth of the poet, the mouth of the prophet, even before he utters it, *per omnia sæcula sæculorum*, world without end.

VII

These considerations, if they have indeed touched on the under-existing nerve that quickens both art and religion, have taken us, perhaps a bit too sweepingly, out of the main line of our subject, and it is time that we return to it, even if that return can be nothing more than a recapitulation, a conclusion, for in fact there is little more to be said. We have seen that poetry and fascism are, with religion, rooted in a deeper archetype in the collective unconscious. We have seen that what fascism cannot be permitted to enforce politically in the modern world must in some way be enacted or it will fester and corrupt; that, apart from religion, the æsthetic way is the most efficacious; that the "solutions" of writers like Lawrence and Eliot and Pound, however objectionable in ideological and political form, are essential to the life of the imagination, and must be given play in our art. We might almost say that fascism occurs when art and religion become so idealized and abstract that the archetype can find no play in the psychic life, and finding none, over-simplifies itself in direct action.

We conclude, therefore, returning to the example with which we began, that since Lawrence-the-Maker and Lawrence-the-Judge are one and the same man, the man knew what he was talking about, that he talked what he knew. His answers are

as crucial as his questions. More importantly, his questions are
met in his answers, because his answer, as we noted, is his art.
For it is apparent that regardless how intensely political might
be an author's intention, the adoption of the mode of poetry
shifts its solution from the political to the archetypal level, from
the areas of action to the areas of contemplation. This is most
apparent in a poem like "Under Ben Bulben". To speak of a fascist rhetoric here is absurd.

With Jeffers however the point is different. He does not
present the same difficulties because, unlike the others, his intentions are not political. This is apparent even in this most
extreme of his poems, "Hellenistics," where, from what we
have seen above, it might seem that however remotely projected into the future, some form of political intent is urged.
Actually, this is not so. For even here, read carefully, it is evident that Jeffers' admonition to the children of the future is not
the evocation to orgiasm it superficially seems to be. He is saying, on the contrary, that *since* this is what you are going to do,
since orgiasm is your need and the need is obviously going to
grow as man's objective life becomes more sterile, more security
threatened, then for God's sake try to eliminate the corruptions
that ruined it in the past. Avoid the doctrinaire. Because the
doctrinaire is the agency of security. And it is security that
threatens the spirit. Go backward to Dionysos or go forward to
him, but for God's sake go in freedom. Keep your exultance
clean.

As for himself, he will do neither. He prefers solitude, and
wishes we did too. For him contemplation lies beyond any kind
of orgiastic participation. It lies in solitude. But he has no hope
of that for the majority of men, they have never desired it, and
are not apt to seek it now. He sees their pitiful orgiastic needs,
the Dionysian uprush that is emerging out of the abstractness
of modern life, out of blind abstractness, the white light of the

ideal, and dragging it down to frenzy and chanting. And he gives them his blessing, his priestly blessing, as poet. And he will be torn by them. Out of his own mouth, as was Dionysos their god, their priest, he will suffer dismemberment. As was Orpheus, their poet, priest of the word. For men need sacrifice. They cry out for the blood of priests and poets, because this blood is efficacious. This blood, given or taken, when it is spilled, really changes the heart. It really makes the world new.

6

The Far=Cast Spear

An introduction to a study of *The Women at Point Sur*,
this paper was written to refocus attention on
Jeffers' central masterpiece and to reverse
the prevalent feeling that it, of all his
poems, is least successful.

> *I sometime*
> *Shall fashion images great enough to face him*
> *A moment and speak while they die. These*
> *   here have gone mad:*
> *But stammer the tragedy you crackled vessels.*
> —The Women at Point Sur

In my paper on Jeffers' fine meditative poem "Post Mortem" I sought to show how a conscious, powerfully deployed artistry belied the charges of crudity and shapelessness often levelled against his work. But because many critics concede to Jeffers' shorter poems a certain controlled sufficiency of form (even Yvor Winters acknowledged that "Hurt Hawks II" is "quite fine"), it might be argued that such detailed examination of a carefully selected minor poem really offers little toward the rehabilitation of Jeffers as a major American writer. The decline of Jeffers' reputation, once so emphatic, was occasioned, we are told, by a reconsideration of his larger narratives, wherein the themes of excess and violence are chiefly met. From this point of view, only when these narratives are shown to be examples of fine poetic art in their own right can any real restoration of Jeffers' reputation be entertained. I propose, therefore, to take up the most difficult and forbidding of all his poems, not indeed to submit it to the same density of textual analysis as was attempted with "Post Mortem," but still to consider it with sufficient attention to arrive at some understanding of its specific weight, its intrinsic substance. As a beginning, two sections will be devoted to the critical problem. Before taking up the powerful assault of the hostile, it seems best to consider the reservations of those who think of themselves as his friends. Even for them *The Women At Point Sur*, from the moment of its inception, was a stumbling block.

I

When on June 30, 1927, Jeffers' monumental narrative was formally published, his career, cresting rapidly after a belated

beginning, was at that crucial point best described as "penulti-
mate." Forty years old, the poet had waited long. When recognition came, it came dramatically — he was suddenly the kind
of dark horse sensation every obscure poet dreams of but never
becomes. Not only had the privately printed *Tamar* scored an
underground success among the intelligentsia—a fact so im-
probable, given the conditions of the book's production and
distribution, that it can only be called a miracle — but a year
later the trade edition bearing the imprint of a leading *avant-
garde* publisher, fortified with strong new work and retitled
Roan Stallion, Tamar and Other Poems, had cut a swath like
a scorched earth campaign through the studios and bistros of
Greenwich Village to climb to a smashing success in the national
press. Now, on this new eve of publication, the iron that
Tamar had heated was glowing red in the banked coals of *Roan
Stallion*. Another triumph would make it white hot. Could the
sensational promise of the first great breakthrough be crystallized? Or was this new poet merely one of those meteoric flashes
that emerge, given decades like the twenties, to burn out with
one sensational book and never be seen again? For the poet's
admirers the moment had all the suspense of the silent film
serials with which Hollywood inveigled Saturday's ground-
lings back to the box office. They had announced his emergence
with the most extravagant praise, and they had to have him
follow through, clinch his place among the positive voices of
his time. As for the poet himself, we do not know his mood.
The image he gave, ensconced in his stone tower, going his own
way with glyptic unconcern, has truth, certainly, but hardly the
whole of it. There are signs that behind the great stone face he,
too, was human.

   The Women at Point Sur moved into this situation of extreme
suspense in a way that no one could have predicted. The book
had everything that was expected: the same unreal landscape,

the same obsessive mood, the same blasted men and lustful women. True, there were none of the beautiful, grave, somehow reassuring lyrics that had tempered the flickering narrative violence of the first two books. But that fact itself ought to increase the impact, for this work had bulk; it stood alone between its covers and demanded that it and nothing else be reckoned with.

And yet what should have been a smash — if incest, suicide and violence had done it before, then incest, rape and violence could do it again — was only a wounding, agonized deflation. Nor can it be said that simply an over-ripe inflation was mercifully punctured. The book was not a *gaffe*. It stood too powerfully apart for that. The incredible power, the unfailing passion, the massive running thrust of sheer language driven beyond the extreme any language ought to be forced to go — all the impact that the *Roan Stallion* volume had promised was certainly there, and greater, and more of it, and more inclusive. But . . . *What did it mean*? That was the question. What was it all about? Men who had prayed for a smash like they had never prayed for grace had the awful feeling that their prayers were answered. But God, who had not deigned to shake their hearts, had, with this doomed appalling book, gone them something better. He had kicked them in the teeth.

And the reviews, when they came, registered it. They carried the bewildered responses of bewildered men. The appearance of the hoped-for masterpiece that would clinch the achievement, that would conclusively vindicate what they had asserted in the speakeasies and proclaimed in the press, must now be postponed. But when metal is glowing delay, any delay, is fatal, and so it was with Jeffers. The great moment passed. Though the work that followed would reassure many, *Point Sur*, coming when the iron was cherry and crisping for the hammer, the crucial stroke that seals prestige forever — *Point Sur* was cold water. From then on, and forever afterward, what hung over

the name and the fame of Robinson Jeffers was not an exclama-
tion point but a question mark. No matter with what restraint
he might limn the frame of Cawdor; no matter how sensitively,
how tenderly he might delineate the heart of the loving shep-
herdess, there stood, always, in the mind of the reader, that
mad minister Barclay, glaring out of the buckeye thickets of
the imagination and the memory, his eyes glazed, his lips
frothed, and his exposed genitals, obscene, revolting, stained
with the blood of his own daughter's virtue.

The setback, for all the monumental aloofness that kept him
immured in his tower by the sea, must have touched the poet to
the quick. In the work that followed, among the shorter lyrics,
those briefer revealments in which his personal feelings, as
distinct from the cosmic vision of his narratives, were so sensitively expressed, would come one called "The Bird With the
Dark Plumes." I think it reveals more than the poet meant it to.
There is a high exultance in the hurt, but for all the exultance,
can the hurt be hid?

> The bird with the dark plumes in my blood,
> That never for one moment, however I patched my truces,
> Consented to make peace with the people,
> It is pitiful now to watch her pleasure in a breath of tempest
> Breaking the sad promise of spring.
> Are these that morose hawk's wings, vaulting, a mere mad swallow's,
> The snow-shed peak, the violent precipice?
> Poor outlaw that would not value their praise do you prize
>   their blame?
> "Their liking," she said, "was a long creance,
> But let them be kind enough to hate me, that opens the sky."
> It is almost as foolish my poor falcon
> To want hatred as to want love; and harder to win.

The long creance is a string fastened to a falcon's heel to prevent
her escape during training. By a strange irony it also carries the
meaning of belief, of faith. Was the snapped string that opened
the sky the faithlessness of his friends?

For the doubt, the bafflement, the ambivalence, the shock that greeted *Point Sur* has never really lifted from it. There would come the outright attacks of enemies, and that is normal, that clearly is to be expected. But the doubt, the *embarrassment* of one's friends and admirers is a thing that cuts a man where no armor protects him. The *gall* of their apologies! Ten years later when he compiled his *Selected Poetry* he kept only a page from *Point Sur*, but in the introduction he mentions, proudly, his foremost work, and he mentions it first: "*The Women at Point Sur* seems to me — in spite of grave faults — the most inclusive, and poetically the most intense of any of my poems." And then, stiff-lipped: "it is omitted from this selection because it is the least understood and least liked, and because it is the longest." In his heart the poet receives the rejection of the best he has done by the best of his friends as a kind of killing disbelief, a profound failure of faith. He lives Christ's gaze on Judas. Oh, he can forgive the wound — seventy times seven, if need be. But he can never be healed of it.

II

To begin, then, I want to take up the reaction to *Point Sur* of Jeffers' admirers—not the initial bafflement but the considered judgment of later commentators. For by looking at the reservations his friends have for the poem we may be able to bring into focus what the total attacks of his opponents only obscure. If we can settle with these difficulties, the thrusts of detractors can be met in their own way; our ground will, at least, have been cleared of ambiguities.

"Of all Jeffers' work," writes Lawrence Clark Powell, in his pioneer study of the Californian, "it is this long and complex poem which most puzzles the general reader," and goes on:

> The poem's weakness, as I see it, lies in its lack of balance: climaxes of lust and terror are superimposed until the reader's sensibilities are

nearly benumbed, [but] the poem is strung on a loom of beautiful
language which, at times, rises to exalted heights.

Carpenter writes:

> The most extreme (and the least successful) of all Jeffers' narrative
> poems focused most sharply on the problem of violence . . . Extreme
> literary violence resulted in complete literary failure.

And Squires remarks:

> Whatever rhetorical success the poem has, it fails to realize the mani-
> fold hopes that Jeffers entertained. Even as a study in abnormal psy-
> chology it is not successful, for the psychology with its excessively
> Freudian stratagems has merely the effect of mechanizing and de-
> feating the characters.

Only Rudolph Gilbert seems to have accepted *Point Sur* without
reservation, seeing in its hero a figure powerful enough to stand
beside the tormented giants of Shakespeare and Dostoevski
and Ibsen:

> The Rev. Dr. Barclay, the protagonist of *The Women at Point Sur*, is
> a literary type worthy to be ranked with Hamlet, Ivan Karamazov,
> and Brand. Dr. Barclay is a man who in the end is powerless before
> the unconquerable power of biological life. He may be likened to
> Oedipus trying to solve the riddle of the sphinx, a universal human-
> ity seeking itself and destroyed by itself, like Hamlet in despair over
> the external fixity of things, Karamazov martyred by doubt and a
> great sin, Brand, bruised and bleeding, wishing "everything and
> nothing," eternal *Christus futurus* and *homo futurus* in conflict.

> In Dr. Barclay Jeffers has created a symbol of the truth, terribly real-
> ized, that the individual cannot exist singly for himself alone, like a
> Lucretian atom, but is of "the mold to break away from." In this
> tragic poem Jeffers has touched, as does Pascal, the void outside hu-
> man existence. In no other poem does his fancy reach such an emin-
> ence of unendurable height. The deep *Weltschmerz*, the blind race of
> man in fetters, is heroically conceived as it might have been by Mi-
> chael Angelo or Beethoven. Here the Nietzschean *"Will zur Nacht"*
> becomes, through poetic vision, a prophesy. A new note is struck—
> "God thinks through action"— suggesting Aquinas's "Intellectus

igitur et voluntas in Deo non sunt ut potentiæ, sed solum ut actio-
nes." The Blakean "God is no more" in Jeffers has been replaced
with "humanity is no more." God alone must be realized; even sacrifice of the human, the womanly, may become necessary to this realization.

If I have permitted Professor Gilbert to speak at such length,
despite a certain efflorescence of expression and a sweeping ec-
lecticism of reference, it is in order to place Barclay where I
think he belongs, among his tortured peers in world literature.
This, of course, has been specifically denied. Mrs. Monjian
points out that the difference between Dostoevski's Raskolnikov and a typical Jeffers protagonist, Margrave, is that

> while the young Russian suffers and repents so that at the novel's
> end he shines forth a finer-edged human being, Margrave doggedly
> believes in his murder's justification until he hangs himself to spare
> himself . . .

> Since many of Jeffers' tragedies are rooted in Greek tragedy, it seems
> evident that he admires these great plays from which Aristotle made
> his observations. And therefore it seems justifiable to apply some of
> Aristotle's derived principles to the dramatic narratives.

She is forced to conclude that "on Aristotelian terms Jeffers does
not succeed." If this is not wholly true, for Horace Gregory and
Marya Zaturenska have stated flatly of *Roan Stallion* that "no
narrative poem written by an American during the twentieth
century is a better example of the classical rules of unity," it is
nevertheless true enough to serve as a generalization. The real
question is, taken simply as a judgment, what is it worth?

III

For H.D.F. Kitto, it isn't worth much. His book *Greek Tragedy*
makes it clear that as far as Aristotelian terms were concerned,
the great Greek tragedians themselves are not infrequently
found to deviate.

We may now inquire what is the relation of Aristotle's theory to
Aeschylus. The answer is, roughly, None whatever. Aristotle's tragic hero, who must be neither good nor bad, but average (or a little
better) and 'like' us, is the Sophoclean hero who in himself prefigures the human tragedy, all of it. He must be a blend of good and
bad, strong and weak, or his ruin will mean nothing. The Aeschylean
hero, who is not intended to sum up and typify in his own breast the
tragic strength and weakness of man, need not be a blend and therefore cannot be 'like us'; he must be only the sinner, with so much
characterization as to make him intelligible. He is, notwithstanding
this, far from being the completely wicked man in whose downfall
Aristotle refused to be interested; he is not a complete man at all, for
we see (as of course in Sophocles too) only that part of him that belongs to the drama, and it is a single part; and, what is more important, he acts not from evil motives but from moral blindness.

Of special interest to the problem of Jeffers:

Since the Aeschylean hero is so single-minded we need to be careful
with the doctrine of hamartia. In Aristotle's theory this is the flaw,
be it great or small, moral or intellectual, without which the hero
would not have fallen nor his character have been a tragic one. The
hybris of Xerxes or Agamemnon is not this at all; it is something
without which these heroes would not exist; *it is all of them that
matters.* [Italics mine.]

Or, in regard to certain dramatic sequences in *Prometheus
Bound:*

The choice of these and the order of their appearance is not arbitrary,
but it is by no means inevitable; we cannot say that they come . . .
by Aristotle's law of inevitable or probable sequence. It would be
possible and just as natural for Io to appear before Oceanus — but
this does not involve Aristotle's censure of plays in which scenes
could be transposed without making any difference. Aristotle's rule
is not valid here. There is a law, *but it is one of increasing tension,*
not of 'natural' or logical sequence . . .

Wherever we look therefore in Medea we find that Euripides differs
from Aristotle's theory and Sophocles' practice, and that not merely
on the surface but radically . . .

> Medea is drawn stark as the strongest possible impersonation of this force; balance of character is necessarily denied her . . . Euripides is not asking us to sympathize with her . . . but to understand her, to understand that such things are, that Medeas and Jasons exist, poetically if not actually . . .

Or:

> He is presenting to us his tragic conception that the passions and unreason to which humanity is subject are its greatest scourge. This implies no tragic interlock between character and situation; the situation is nothing but the setting for the outburst of unreason, the channel along which it rushes. What matters now is not that the situation must be convincing and illuminating, not even that the heroine must be convincing as a person; but that her passion must be, in however extreme a form, a fundamental and familiar one. If Medea is in this sense true, we shall not stay to object that she is not likely.

"Lest we be tempted," Kitto says, "to think that these [differences] are only casual licenses taken by the poet which can, with luck, be explained away, we ought to observe how fundamental is the divergence between the poet and the philosopher here."

It is a divergence as old as man's heart. Mark Van Doren, who found Jeffers with *Tamar* and lost him with *Point Sur*, defines, in his famous essay on the *Iliad*, "the main art a poet must learn":

> the art of standing at the right distance from his matter, of keeping the right relation to it, and of using, along with the knowledge he brings, the knowledge he gains while he goes. With the poet, as with the historian, the position he takes is everything, and we shall not believe him unless he maintains it.

Shall we not? If position is everything, then the minor poet is the equal of the major one, for each determines his own place. Longfellow maintains, with the historian, his distance from *Evangeline* with infinitely more success than Shakespeare does from Hamlet, Milton from Satan, or Goethe from Faust, and still we do not believe him. But Kitto reminds us:

> Euripides sacrifices. . . .external tidiness to directness of expression, being in this truly Greek; for surely the greatness of all Greek art lies not in its ability to achieve beauty of form (never the first aim of the great artist), but in its absolute sincerity to the underlying idea.

It is this "directness of expression," this passion, this total commitment to the underlying motive, which I wish to accent as the key to the achievement of Robinson Jeffers.

IV

For the correspondence upon which Gilbert identified Barclay with the other suffering heroes of our literature was made upon an equally processive stripping away, a reduction through the accumulation of experience to the essential flaw of his humanity, the flaw that is not accidental at all, but precisely *all of him that matters*. This processive stripping away, this reduction of excrescence upon excrescence to the point of annihilation, produces a different form and style than the one validated by Aristotle, ordained as it was to a point of view which assumed a metaphysic centered upon an abiding principle of limit in the cosmos. W. Norris Clarke, S.J., in a study of the origins of Greek philosophical attitudes, writes:

> The inability of the early Greek thinkers to transcend material categories or to distinguish between philosophy and natural science, their growing preoccupation with astronomical problems, and the very manner in which they framed their fundamental problem, "What is the first principle *out of which* all things are formed?" gradually led them — if not Anaximander, at least his successor — to identify the infinite with the indeterminate, formless substratum or raw material of the universe, the primeval chaos of matter in itself, as yet unperfected by the limit of form. Emerging out of it and opposed to it was the finished, or perfect cosmos, formed, limited and intelligible.

Thus, for Plato and Aristotle both,

> the principle of limitation is consistently identified with number,
> form, idea, and being, as the source of intelligibility and perfection.
> The principle of illimitation, on the other hand, is identified with the
> formlessness and indeterminacy of pure matter as such and there-
> fore with "otherness" or nonbeing, as the source of unintelligibility
> and imperfection.

But by the time of Plotinus, five centuries later,

> the emergence of the new notion of infinity seems to have been
> provoked not by any internal progress of philosophical speculation
> by itself, but by the impact of the mystery religions of the East, now
> infiltrating the Roman Empire on all sides. The latter brought with
> them a new notion of divinity, a divinity of power and mystery,
> master of the limitless spaces of the heavens, discovered by the new
> Syrian astronomy, above all rational human concepts, but with
> whom the believer could enter into salvivic personal union by mysti-
> cal or other non-rational means.

This transcendental acquisition from the East must have found
a fertile ground in the Dionysian element in Greek culture,
which of course has come down in mythology, ritual and drama, if not in philosophy, as itself a valid element of the divine,
and which actually produced the creative tension in Greek
sensibility, until the triumph of Rome, with its passion for order
and law, re-emphasized the rational in the philosophical heritage. Nevertheless, the underlying tension, inherited and passed
forward, achieved its highest expression in Christianity, where
the torn God of Dionysos Zagreus, the transcendental God of
the mystery cults, and the "rational" God of Plato and Aristotle found their ultimate synthesis and resolution. But the
Protestant insistence on a dichotomy between reason and faith
led, after the Enlightenment, to the triumph of a dissociated
rationality, until the cleavages between these psychic dimen-
sions forced that fracturing so markedly defined and deplored
in modern man. It is within the dimension of this culturally

received, yet rationally discounted cleavage in the collective
psyche, that Jeffers, as well as every other modern poet, wrote.

As far as his Greek heritage was concerned, Jeffers, of course,
spoke from both the Dionysian and Apollonian perspectives.
Squires has shown how his narratives divide in formation between these two poles, which he identifies as "the saga formula
and the classical, the diffuse and the unified." For him, the
"unified" is typified by *Roan Stallion*. The exemplar of the
"diffuse" however, is typified by *Point Sur*, his judgment of
which we have already seen. But if my insight is correct, the
cleavage goes back to the crisis in Greek culture, between the
earlier concept of the divine as *limit* over against the mytholog-
ically-intuited apprehension of chaos as itself divine, and the
later, grafted-on, orientally-derived concept of the divine as
Infinite. It is with some such background in mind that I hope to
redress Squires' judgment, and establish that the "diffuse" not
the "unified" is the keystone of Jeffers' achievement. My intuition is that the more deeply seated Dionysian element in his
psyche enables him to commit a more powerfully centered voli-
tional resource to processively breaking down the culturally-
affixed limits of his figures, and that intensity, not outline, is
the key to his genius. If it is true that his sense of form is provisional, in that he establishes it in order to transcend it, it is no
less true that its establishment is quite adequate to the tasks of
transcendence, and his singular acuity of visual concretization
is crucial to this purpose. I believe that the superiority of intensity was for him validated by the fact that his Christian-ori-
ented religious intuition enabled him to conceive of an infinite
God greater than any series of limitations the Greek concept of
the finite, seated in his culture, was able to bring against it.

For the mind of every man is balanced upon the creative tension within him of conceptual mediation between the opposed
polarities of the finite and the infinite, the essential and the

existential. The exact equation between them is responsible for
the basic human types, which, in æsthetics, constitute the classical and the romantic temperaments. R.V. Collingwood has
accented the difference between classicism and romanticism as
a distinction between concern for craft, for making, and concern
for the subject. And indeed, were it not obvious in his work, Jeffers has affirmed the "romantic" solution by declaring that "the
poetry is in the subject." If, therefore, it goes without saying
that Jeffers is a true "Dionysian," it must be insisted, against
the critical prejudice of our time, that his transcendent greatness above contemporary formulas is assured, not denied, by
this fact. For that he has powerful Apollonian elements within
him is equally obvious. The enormous energies this tension
generated does indicate the preponderance, the ultimate accent,
of the expansiveness over the restraint, but my effort will be to
show that the expansion is centered and directed, that the
powerful forces of restraint in Jeffers, and in his greatest poem,
retain the focus within which that expansion takes place, and
that the end result of this process is not diffusion but a true
expansion of consciousness; not despair but exaltation; that the
annihilation of man is essentially a symbolic annihilation of
egoism; and that Jeffersian nihilism is a cancelling out of the
contingent only to get through to the incomparable splendor of
the Absolute. In order to achieve this he employs the right hand
and the left with equal force, focussing the intellect with the
right hand of the imagination, and transcending its projectives
in the left hand of the will, constellated in the insuperable tor-
rent of his sound.

For the contemplation of this denouement, this cancelling
out of contingency, does leave the reader not with hopelessness
but with self-knowledge and the birth of understanding. And
when we finish with Barclay we are able to say, of certain tendencies within us carried to their term, "Now I see," and seeing

are chastened and appeased. In approaching this task we have
touched on the misgivings and bewilderment of Jeffers' friends,
his keenest apologists; before we proceed, however, we have to
meet the objection not of those who think the best of him but
of those who think the worst.

V

The worst was written by Yvor Winters, and it came only three
or four years after *Point Sur* was published. Nor has its influence
passed, as instanced by this recent testament from the pen of
Kenneth Rexroth, who in recourse to it acknowledges perhaps
his only appeal to the authority of a New Critic:

> Many years ago [Jeffers'] only serious rival to the title of "Cali-
> fornia's leading poet" wrote an essay on him in the *Hound and Horn*,
> later substantially reprinted in the book *In Defense of Reason*. It was
> one of the most devastating attacks in modern criticism and Jeffers'
> reputation, then at its height, never recovered, but entered a slow
> decline.

It goes without saying that for many discriminating readers the
judgment still stands. I shall quote Winters' attack at sufficient
length to register the full measure of its condemnation.

> *The Women at Point Sur* is a perfect laboratory of Mr. Jeffers'
> philosophy. Barclay, an insane divine, preaches Mr. Jeffers' religion,
> and his disciples, acting upon it, become emotional mechanisms,
> lewd and twitching conglomerations of plexi, their humanity an-
> nulled. Human experience, in these circumstances, having necessarily
> and according to the doctrine no meaning, there can be and is no
> necessary sequence of events: every act is equivalent to every other;
> every act is at the peak of hysteria; most of the incidents could be
> shuffled around into varying sequences without violating anything
> save, perhaps, Mr. Jeffers' private sense of their relative intensity.
> Since the poem is his, of course, such a private sense is legitimate
> enough; the point is that this is not a narrative, nor a dramatic, but
> a lyrical criterion. A successful lyrical poem of one hundred and
> seventy-five pages is unlikely, for the essence of lyrical expression is

concentration; but it is at least theoretically possible. The difficulty is that the lyric achieves its effect by the generalization of emotion (that is, by the separation of the emotion from the personal history that gives rise to it in actual concrete experience) and by the concentration of expression. Narrative can survive in a measure without concentration, or intensity of detail, provided the narrative logic is detailed and compelling, as in the case of Balzac, though it is only wise to add that this occurs most often in prose.

Now Mr. Jeffers, as I have pointed out, has abandoned narrative logic with the theory of ethics, and he has never achieved, in addition, a close and masterly style. His writing is loose, turgid, and careless; like most anti-intellectualists, he relies on his feelings alone and has no standard of criticism for them outside of themselves. There are occasional good flashes in his poems, and to these I shall return later, but they are very few, are very limited in their range of feeling and in their subject matter, and they are very far between. Mr. Jeffers has no remaining method of sustaining his lyric, then, other than the employment of an accidental (i.e., non-narrative) chain of anecdotes (i.e., details that are lyrically impure); his philosophical doctrine and his artistic dilemma alike decree that these shall be anecdotes of hysteria. By this method Mr. Jeffers continually *lays claim* to a high pitch of emotion which has no narrative support (that is, support of the inevitable accumulation of experience), nor lyrical support (that is, support of the intense perception of pure, or transferable, emotion), which has, in short, no support at all, and which is therefore simply unmastered and self-inflicted hysteria.

The strategy here of course is two-pronged: it strikes at both ends and means. By a simplifying process of reduction the end is contemptuously dismissed, and any real correction must wait upon the complete emergence of those ends as the poem itself unfolds. However, Squires has scored Winters' oversimplifications:

I wish to share Mr. Winters' reservations about *The Women at Point Sur* as a work of art, but not his confusions about it as doctrine. Barclay, as I have already taken pains to demonstrate, does not preach Jeffers' "religion," but the opposite of his religion. Nor do Barclay's "disciples" (if by "disciples" Mr. Winters means the other main characters in the narrative) act upon it. They are, as a matter of fact, only faintly aware of what Barclay is up to and they go pretty much their own ways. They are indeed "lewd and twitching" (it is impossible to improve on Mr. Winters' diction when he is inspired by indignation), but they are connected with Jeffers' creed only by a relationship of antipathy.

Anyone who has found Winters' criticism of Jeffers "devastating" may select the adjective he chooses to describe what this does to one prong of Winters' attack.

But it is the other prong behind which Winters mounts his chief offensive, and it is hard to answer, for by an arbitrary restriction of sanction to two closely defined methodologies, narrative and lyric, the critic is enabled to have it both ways. He concludes that since the poet does not write "pure" versions of either, his work must fail. The reply of Jeffers' apologists has chiefly been to expand the available categories, but this has not gone well, for Jeffers' longer poems are commonly called narratives, and it is hard to object to Winters' employment of the term and yet avoid relapsing frequently into its use.

Still, it is apparent that Jeffers' "narratives" do not move in the way that Winters defines the movement of narrative. Amos Wilder, trying for a more satisfactory category, writes: "The point is that these poems ordinarily should not be read or judged as narratives. [Yet he cannot call them anything else throughout his study.] They are hymns of salvation and interest lies not in any cogent sequence of human interest...but in the constant tension between the life of man and the goal beyond it." To call *Point Sur* a hymn of salvation is I think true enough in the highest and most acute reading of the poem, but not very serviceable in critical discussion.

Frederic Carpenter calls the narratives "modern myths" and this is more helpful:

> Conceived in terms of myth — rather than of tragedy, or of fiction, or of philosophy — Jeffers' long poems can be described and judged

by their own "singular" virtues or faults, rather than by the lack of virtues to which they never pretended. The particular qualities of his individual poems appear clearly when described in these terms, and the separate poems fall into definable groups. The changes of form and psychology which have marked his creative career assume a meaningful pattern. If these changes in his poetic conceptions were not always for the good, at least they were not capricious, but were directed by the logic (or the illogic) of modern myth.

The difficulty here is that while the term *narrative* is a purely formal designation, the word *myth* relates more to psychological attitude than to form. A narrative is a tale, a story, and unquestionably *Point Sur* is that. But a myth as a category is more a habit of mind. Heinrich Zimmer quotes Nietzsche:

> "It is not true", says Nietzsche, "that there is some hidden thought or idea at the bottom of the myth, as some in a period of civilization that has become artificial have put it, but the myth itself is a *kind or style of thinking*. It imparts an idea of the universe, but does it in the sequence of events, actions, and sufferings."

Zimmer goes on:

> This is why we may look into it as into a mirror or fountain full of hints and prophecies, telling us what we are and how we should behave amidst the bewildering sequences of surprising events and happenings that are our common lot . . . Myth is the sole and spontaneous image of life itself in its flowing harmony and mutually hostile contrarieties, in all the polyphony and harmony of their contradictions. Therein lies its inexhaustible power.

This we feel is true, but from a formal point of view it does not help us. It all could be asserted, for instance, of "Art." How are we to meet the charge that so long as myth deals with "the sequence of events" it must be judged by the law of narrative, "the inevitable accumulation of experience," as Mr. Winters defines it?

The solution is this. While myth does indeed proceed by virtue of the "inevitable accumulation of experience" the sequence is not governed by rational but by symbolic criteria. Myth emerged before art, that is to say, before the direct application of individual consciousness to æsthetic form. With the triumph of reason in the evolution of consciousness symbolic referents fell into the background, became mere adjuncts to the main course of æsthetic development. But with the crisis of reason in modern times, and the opening of the unconscious, symbolic correspondences once again emerged, not on the collective level as with archaic myth, but on the individual level, as discernible in the scenarios of modern dreams no less than in the modal evolution of modern narrative forms — flashback, stream of consciousness, etc. It is the task of the critic to expose the process of symbolic sequence which underlies the narrative action, no matter how apparently "anecdotal," and it must be done by recourse to a theory of symbolism solidly based on psychological reality rather than on the conscious deployment of classical mythical phenomena.

Thus it is disappointing to find Carpenter relying on an obsolete definition of myth as "an imaginary story usually concerning deities and demi-gods" and thinking of the characters of myth as "primarily personifications of natural forces." This leads him to posit a dichotomy between the "mythical" and the "modern" psychology in Jeffers' characters, a dichotomy which he feels simply throws the reader off step. All this is not true. Whether ancient or modern, the characters of myth are essentially archetypal projections. Barclay is not a personification of a natural force, he is an embodiment of the archetype of the redeemer. That Jeffers understands the nature of archetypes is shown full well in one of his first narratives, *Roan Stallion*:

> *The fire threw up figures*
> *And symbols meanwhile, racial myths formed and dissolved in it,*
> *   the phantom rulers of humanity*
> *That without being are yet more real than what they are born of, and*

without shape, shape that which makes them:
The nerves and the flesh go by shadowlike, the limbs and the lives
   shadowlike, these shadows remain, these shadows
To whom temples, to whom churches, to whom labors and wars,
   visions and dreams are dedicate.

The method is a direct recourse to the subjective interiority upon which archetypal situation is grounded. Nor are mythical events mere anecdotes. Rather by a shift in perspective all anecdotes can be seen to participate, if they have any interest at all, in some underlying archetypal stimulus. Because the atmosphere of archetypal situation is mythical rather than narrational or lyrical, the poet boldly induces a dimension of psychological suspense, and having secured it moves forward by generating a kind of cyclonic intensification, situation to situation as he proceeds, and develops his intensity by virtue of increase of archetypal pressure. The scenarios of dream and myth follow the same emotional contours, and may not be evaluated by the criteria of logic. They have come into being precisely to afford play to correspondences in depth which the workaday forces of logic could not accommodate. Poetry and art, it is true, proceed closer to the conscious mind, to the reason — if dreams sufficed men would never write poetry — but nevertheless their impetus is sourced in the same origins as those of dream.

For if "narrative" is the rational ordering of explicit events and if "lyric" is the generalization of emotion obtaining between subject and object then myths, visions, dreams, are scenarios of mood. Mood is the psychic dimension that accommodates the hiatus left by a deficiency of reason, or knowledge, in man's perception of phenomena. Its symbolism is not the static, consciously deployed system of referents we find supporting the methodologies of narrative and lyric. Rather it is fluid, it proceeds by an interior qualitative association, but it does not lack "inevitability." For instance, when Barclay enjoys the gross Indian woman Maruca in Chapter VI this act *evokes* his daughter, who symbolizes virginity and purity, in the next chapter. They are not unrelated anecdotes, therefore; they are related by archetypal accommodation, each evoking, and subsequently yielding to, another. The processive determination is that of psychological suspension, symbolic accommodation, and, if the poet is good, cumulative intensification.

This intensification, furthermore, escapes the charge of hysteria, "emotion in excess of motive," for here, as in mysticism, emotion is ultimately authenticated not by its motive but by its end. It is Mr. Winters' refusal to understand this end that occasions his indictment of the method. But in this he is typical not only of the poet's opponents but of his advocates as well. I believe that the difficulty the contemporary reader has with the poem is not a failure on Jeffers' part to mount and sustain intensity, not in any "laying claim" to a high pitch of emotion that has no rational support, but in the very direction and term toward which the mounting intensity is inexorably directed, in his version of an Absolute that redeems and justifies the processes leading to it.

Nor can it be said that, however exemplary the term, the underlying compulsions which Jeffers is uncovering are as yet insufficiently assimilated into our consciousness to be fully accessible to the contemporary reader, even the trained reader. No, what continues to shake us about *Point Sur* is the appalling density of psychic atmosphere which its diction, imagery, rhythm, pace and apprehension of phenomena generate. The compulsions are familiar enough: what distinguishes them here is the psychic registration, at once refined and primitive. And this primitivism is achieved by recourse to a duality of direction. First, the term, the holy and terrible presence of the divine as it overshadows the human situation. And second, that terrible presence is achieved by an invocation from the roots of the being of a force outside nature which can only be called *dæ-monic*. And it is a force which is constellated, as in no other Jeffersian work, around the polarity of a single man. Goethe writes:

> The dæmonic character appears in its most *dreadful* form when it stands out dominatingly in some *man*. Such are not always the most remarkable men, either in spiritual quality or natural talents, and they seldom have any goodness of heart to recommend them. But an incredible force goes forth from them and they exercise an incredible power over all creatures, nay, perhaps even over the elements. And who can say how far such an influence may not extend?

It is my contention that no other figure in American literature, not Ahab himself, so powerfully localizes this incredible force as does Jeffers' terrible hero, The Rev. Dr. Barclay.

Thus when Gilbert writes that "Barclay is a man who in the end is powerless before the unconquerable power of biological life" he misses the point at issue behind Barclay's action. And when he writes that "Jeffers' desire to deal solely with the elemental passions tends to mislead the reader into the colder regions of hell which are a paradox of romantic agony; the reader is repelled," he falsifies the actual situation.

I would say rather that Jeffers' heroic necessity to engage the underlying archetype which sources dæmonic action (in Goethe's sense) enables the reader to experience its truth. It is not that the reader is repelled; the important thing is that Jeffers makes it possible to experience *despite*, or, more accurately, precisely *by virtue of*, his repulsion. My hope is, then, to trace the processes of approach insofar as I am able, so that the reader may perceive, as Jeffers himself was driven to perceive, those boiling fountains of inscrutable motivation, those archetypes, and face out what they are. In order to justify this we have already had recourse to the practice of Euripides, for we needed his example to counteract the strictures of contemporary Greek-

ophiles and afford some deliverance from the Iron Maiden of
Aristotle's poetics. This does not imply, however, any real
identity between his own method and that of the Greek tragic
poet.

VI

But if what Jeffers is saying is not what Euripides was saying,
namely, that "passion can be stronger than reason," and which,
as we saw, his commentators generally take him to be saying,
what, then, is his book all about, and how does the example of
Euripides justify his method? It justifies it because in Jeffers' account we indeed do see an overwhelming power at work, with
insuperable intensity and with awesome disintegrating force,
but it is simply that the origin and nature of that force are not
explained by the tension between passion and reason. In deter-
mining what they are I will not have recourse to the list of "intentions" Jeffers spelled out in letters to his friends after the
fact, as it were, when *Point Sur* was under attack. These "intentions" are chiefly responsible for throwing critics off the track
in regard to understanding the poem. The occasion was one of
only two periods in his life when Jeffers lost his detachment,
the other being America's entry into World War II, a much
more serious affair. But in 1927, as I have shown, he was cresting on a wave of renown after years of retardation and unfulfillment, and it is not to be wondered at that he was shaken
when he sensed the collapse of a fame so belatedly won, blast-
ing "the sad promise of spring." Let us go, therefore, directly
to a synopsis of the plot, choosing that of Squires as the most
serviceable. If it is unsympathetic in tone it is the most detailed
and hence closest to our purpose.

> "The Rev. Dr. Barclay" finds suddenly that he has nothing to say to
> his congregation and, deserting his pulpit as well as his wife and
> daughter, he wanders to Point Sur where he takes a room at the

house of Natalia Morhead whose husband has not yet returned from the war. In Morhead's absence his father ("Old Morhead") has become a bedridden cripple, and Natalia has entered into a homosexual relationship with Faith Heriot, a waif who has suffered as a result of male brutality. Barclay ambles about the hills and in his incremental madness attracts disciples. To them he preaches Jeffers' Inhumanism adulterated with his own insanity and repressions. Meanwhile, his "private impurity" compels him to seek sexual liaison with Maruca, an Indian woman. When his daughter, April, arrives with her mother to look after him, he contrives successfully to rape her. April bears the brunt not only of her father's difficulties but also of Rand Morhead's; for Randal returns at length from the war and falls vaguely in love with her. At the same time Faith Heriot becomes jealous of April because she thinks that Natalia's affections have been transferred to her. Eventually April, deranged by her rape and thinking that she is her brother Edward (killed in the war), determines to kill her father but kills herself instead. Barclay wanders on; his hypnotized disciples fall off one by one, and he dies of exhaustion alone in the wilderness.

We will see, in a moment, that the underlying archetype behind Barclay's decisive break with his congregation is the archetype of Renewal, centered deep in the authority of ancient mythological motifs, but before we approach that dimension it is not inappropriate to point out that Barclay's break is not unique, but rather corresponds to a certain dark strain in all revivalism. Ronald Knox, in his book *Enthusiasm*, examines this phenomenon, characteristic of all intense religions, but particularly endemic to Protestantism. In America it led to a virtual paroxysm of schism and proliferation, each hinging on greater and greater charismatic freedom, and progressively foundering on the unconscious forces of sexuality which the sundering invariably unleashed. As a historical phenomenon Barclay's break could be documented many times over in the religious history of America, some of them with actual results hardly less sensational than the dénouement of *Point Sur* itself.

Kitto says of Euripides' *Medea* that "what matters now is not that the situation must be convincing and illuminating, not even that the heroine must be convincing as a person; but that her passion must be, in however extreme a form, *a fundamental and familiar one.*" Thus it cannot be said of *Point Sur* that its situation is implausible. The relationship between revivalism and sexuality is so thoroughly understood by the American mind that it is embedded in our folklore.

From this historical point of view the course of action in *Point Sur* may be seen not as "isolated incidents dependent only upon their author's view as to their relative intensity" but a systematic, step by step, deterioration of ego structure brought about by an unwise attempt to establish direct union with God without an ascesis and without adequate direction, one of the dangers of Protestantism's thrust of centrality back to the primacy of the individual conscience. In fact, it may well be that spiritual directors of the future will place *Point Sur* in the hands of their novices as an object lesson in what happens to the religious enthusiast when he sets out to go it alone. They will point out that, all down the line, Barclay was in the great tradition, from his emphatic break with the world, which, though perhaps too brutal, was nevertheless necessary, to his unfortunate demise, which followed from an unmitigated *hubris*, throwing him among the "Lost," and nullifying all the hope of his great adventure, which was to have secured not only his own place but those of his fellows among the "Saved."

For the step is fraught with extreme danger. What is necessary is a guide, a *guru* or a director of souls as he is known in the West. But when a culture shifts from a sacral orientation to a pluralistic one, the *guru* and the priest alike tend to become mere institutional functionaries, until the fabric of society begins to creak under the strain of its distressed minds, and a new equivalent in time emerges. Joseph L. Henderson, a Jungian psychiatrist, writes in *The Wisdom of the Serpent*:

> This role which has been carried traditionally by the priest is today frequently bestowed upon the psychiatrist as analyst in the language of dreams. I have been represented as a chauffeur, the leader of an archæological expedition, the conductor of an orchestra, and the one who formulates something, a lecturer or teacher all in the spirit of this "messenger of favorable words."As a dentist, doctor, medicine man, male nurse, or priest I may be represented in the role of healer implying that an ordeal to which the dreamer has submitted is brought to a climax in a healing ceremony whether of a practical secular nature or as an act of spiritual enlightenment. The reader will no doubt be able to supply from literature and drama many more examples of this figure acting as an intermediary between the suffering initiate and his experience of the death which may or may not lead to a rebirth; for example, the role of Thoth in the myth of Isis and Horus, Virgil in the *Divina Commedia* as the guide to Dante, Hermes as the guide of Aeneas in the *Aeneid*, Heracles as messenger to the underworld in the *Alcestis*. It was not unintentional that T. S. Eliot patterned Reilly, the psychiatrist in *The Cocktail Party*, upon this aspect of Heracles as a semi heroic, trickster-figure enabled by his mercurial nature to act as mediator between the two worlds, conscious and unconscious. As we trace him back to more primitive levels we find him represented as the tribal medicine man identified with the animal as totem, who is known, whether in animal or human garb, as Master of Initiation.

Without such a guide we have a total succumbing to what Jung calls the *mana-personality*, of which Barclay is certainly an outstanding example, a virtual case history. Jung writes:

> Historically, the mana-personality evolves into the hero and the godlike being, whose earthly form is the priest . . . But insofar as the ego apparently draws to itself the power belonging to the anima, the ego does become a mana-personality. This development is an almost regular phenomenon. I have never yet seen a fairly advanced development of this kind where at least a temporary identification with the archetype of the mana-personality did not take place. It is the most natural thing in the world that this should happen, for not

only does one expect it oneself, but everybody else expects it too. One can scarcely help admiring oneself a little for having seen more deeply into things than others, and the others have such an urge to find a tangible hero somewhere, or a superior wise man, a leader and father, some undisputed authority, that they build temples to little tin gods with the greatest promptitude and burn incense at the altars. This is not just the lamentable stupidity of idolaters incapable of judging for themselves, but a natural psychological law which says that what has once been will always be in the future. And so it will be, unless consciousness puts an end to the naive concretization of primordial images. I do not know whether it is desirable that consciousness should alter the eternal laws; I only know that occasionally it does alter them, and that this measure is a vital necessity for some people — which, however, does not always prevent these same people from setting themselves up on the father's throne and making the old rule come true. It is indeed hard to see how one can escape the sovereign power of the primordial images.

In Barclay we have an example of the man who, utterly without guide himself, yet, seized up in the mana-personality, presumes to guide others. From the historical point of view, his demise could be charted over and over. From the mythological one, the case is more complex, more awesome, and incomparably more interesting. In order to chart it we must have recourse to a more specific text. I propose to use for this purpose Joseph Campbell's *The Hero With a Thousand Faces*, an analysis, with reference to mythology and depth psychology, of the hero archetype as the fundamental agency of psychic and religious renewal. This he calls the "monomyth." Using Campbell's scheme as a guide, we can at least begin with Barclay and see what he is about. If we cannot end with him, it is because Campbell charts the course of the hero through its risks to success, while Jeffers charts it to failure. The ends are diverse, but the motivation the same.

VII

"The standard path of the mythological adventure of the hero," writes Campbell, "is a magnification of the formula represented in the rites of passage: *separation — initiation — return:*"

> *A hero ventures forth from the world of common day into a region of supernatural wonder: fabulous forces are there encountered and a decisive victory is won: the hero comes back from this mysterious adventure with the power to bestow boons on his fellow man.*

> Prometheus ascended to the heavens, stole fire from the gods, and descended. Jason sailed through the Clashing Rocks into a sea of marvels, circumvented the dragon that guarded the Golden Fleece, and returned with the fleece and the power to wrest his rightful throne from a usurper. Aeneas went down into the underworld, crossed the dreadful river of the dead, threw a sop to the three-headed watchdog Cerberus, and conversed, at last, with the shade of his dead father. All things were unfolded to him: the destiny of souls, the destiny of Rome, which he was about to found, "and in what wise he might avoid or endure every burden." He returned through the ivory gate to his work in the world.

Campbell then describes the legend of the Buddha, how the young prince Gautama set forth secretly from his father's palace, endured all the trials of adversity, and at last found enlightenment:

> Then he doubted whether his message could be communicated, and he thought to retain the wisdom for himself; but the god Brahma descended from the Zenith to implore that he should become the teacher of gods and men. The Buddha was thus persuaded to proclaim the path. And he went back into the cities of men where he moved among the citizens of the world, bestowing the inestimable boon of the knowledge of the Way.

"The Old Testament," continues Campbell, (in an observation of special interest for us, because Powell notes that he saw a typescript of *Point Sur* in which Jeffers had labelled Barclay's apotheosis on the mountain as "the Mount Sinai scene")

> records a comparable deed in its legend of Moses, who, in the third

month of the departure of Israel out of the land of Egypt, came with
his people into the wilderness of Sinai; and there Israel pitched their
tents over against the mountain. And Moses went up to God, and
the Lord called unto him from the mountain. The Lord gave to him
the Tables of the Law and commanded Moses to return with these
to Israel, the people of the Lord.

"As we shall see," he summarizes, "whether presented in the
vast, almost oceanic images of the Orient, in the vigorous narratives of the Greeks, or in the majestic legends of the Bible, the
adventure of the hero normally follows the pattern of the nu-
clear unit above described: a separation from the world, a
penetration to some source of power, and a life-enhancing
return."

That Barclay participates in this immemorial pattern is clearly evident in the opening chapter when he breaks with the past
and the present, the conventionalized domain of limitation and
security, and declares for an initiation into a new life. He tells
his congregation:

It is not possible
To know anything while you eat lies: you half-believers, fog-
    people: leave that, wash the eyes, and who knows
Now the earth draws to maturity, has taken the bloody
Initiation of coming of age, you also grown adult
May fish some flaming gleam of knowledge out of the netted ocean,
    run down some deer of perception
In the dark wood . . .
                    It is no alliance
And I am the hunter you shall not run as hounds for: but think, you
    old men, you old women, if one of you
Should stumble over it by chance, you had cleaned the mind that you
    could see it, some instant pebble of perception
Glowing in the dust.

Notice the mythological images of beasts and fishes, of dark
woods, of insignificant pebbles that hold the key to eternal life.
Barclay has himself, before the action begins, already expe-

rienced the reality of the Dark Kingdom, and these images are historically and archetypally its talismans:

> Typical of the circumstances of the call are the dark forest, the great tree, the babbling spring, and the loathly, underestimated appearance of the carrier of the power of destiny.

Barclay's forth-going into the mystic world of the Carmel coast is also in the same tradition.

> This first stage of the mythological journey — which we have designated the "call to adventure"— signifies that destiny has summoned the hero and transferred his spiritual center of gravity from within the pale of his society to a zone unknown. This fateful region of both treasure and danger may be variously represented: as a distant land, a forest, a kingdom underground, beneath the waves, or above the sky, a secret island, lofty mountaintop, or profound dream state; but it is always a place of strangely fluid and polymorphous beings, unimaginable torments, superhuman deeds and impossible delight.

Jeffers then, in directing his creative intention to the problem of a man who sets himself apart and tries to reapproach the essence of inner reality, has himself fallen under the spell of the ancient archetype he has approached, and becomes the instrument of its specification, just as the dreamer who dreams the images which deliver him. Out of his nature-drenched mind the immemorial talismans manifest themselves, and his redeeming hero is on his way.

VIII

But if this sets *Point Sur* in its proper perspective, what it does not do is provide us with the clue to Jeffers' choice of the failure of the legend rather than its accomplishment and success, for it is the failure, not the success, that concerned him.

> *The return and reintegration with society,* which is indispensable to the continuous circulation of spiritual energy into the world, and

which, from the standpoint of the community,is the justification of the long retreat, the hero himself may find the most difficult require-ment of all.

For if he has won through, like the Buddha, to the profound repose of complete enlightenment, there is danger that the bliss of this ex-perience may annihilate all recollection of, interest in, or hope for, the sorrows of the world; or else the problem of making known the way of illumination to people wrapped in economic problems may seem too great to solve.

Are we to believe that this was actually the case with Jeffers, that sometime in the period after the war, but before the writing of *Tamar*, there came to him a mystical experience of such depth and intensity that he could forever after refuse to con-summate the Eternal Return and spend his years justifying his intuition by a series of monumental explanations? From the point of view of Barclay, however, the alternative is obvious:

And on the other hand, if the hero, instead of submitting to all the initiatory tests, has, like Prometheus, simply darted to his goal (by violence, quick device, or luck) and plucked the boon for the world that he intended, then the powers that he has unbalanced may react so sharply that he will be blasted from within and without — cruci-fied, like Prometheus, on the rock of his own violated unconscious.

We are here, without doubt, at the situation of Barclay, hero of Jeffers' blighted myth of renewal. That Jeffers, despite all the negative "intentions" of his after-thought, really saw Barclay as some such Promethean figure is shown, not only by his tacit admission ten years later of the positive achievement of Bar-clay:

I stand near Soberanes Creek, on the knoll over the sea, west of the
  road. I remember
This is the very place where Arthur Barclay, a priest in revolt, pro-
  posed three questions to himself . . .
                              Large timeworn questions no doubt;
  yet he touched his answers, they are not unattainable

but more crucially in his rhetorical commitments, the power and range of participation with which he realizes Barclay's attempt, the kind of emotional identification which critics have long noted in Milton's language when he wrote of Satan, the tell-tale unconscious salute to the abhorred rebel who must carry the author's unconscious rebellion to its term and then be erased in favor of all the conscious norms he has defied.

Actually, when an artist is impelled to write a poem like *Point Sur*, it means that the two polarities within him are locked in a kind of impasse, and he creates the character whose mission it is to resolve it. That side of himself which represents the Institutional—the inherited wisdom of the race, Tradition, the past, its values, ideas, rules and reservations, in short, the Code — gambles that the Hero-Sinner cannot win; while that side of himself which represents pure potentiality — the Charismatic —gambles that he will win, and win through violation. It is not merely that a mind as finely balanced as Jeffers' had to have it both ways; the problem is much deeper. The mere results, what we can call the plot, will represent the Institutional, and will see the hero destroyed — killed off, in fact, to satisfy its norms. But the art, the poetry, all the intuitive *affect* of the writing — the Charismatic — will see to it that he does, somehow, score, and its success is a celebration and a testament to his attainment. So with Barclay: he has to die, to destroy himself as a consequence of his actions. But the dark unknown side of Jeffers has to see that he somehow wins, and all the strange, fiery, violent exultation of the language testifies that he has.

For it is apparent that behind the archetype of renewal reside its various sub-categories, each dominated by a symbolic motif, and each capable of many variations. There is, first of all, the counter archetype of the failure of renewal, the chief motif of which is suicide. But there is also the absolutely crucial intermediate archetype, the one human consciousness always balks

at, and yet the only one really to show the way through, the
one that actually lies beyond the paradigms of success which
Campbell charts. It is the archetype of *renewal through failure.* It is the archetype of the renewal of Christ, who failed
in the fact of his crucifixion and death, and yet who renewed
the world, through that failure, in His resurrection.

It is, obviously, the archetype upon which Jeffers founds the
trial and ordeal of his protagonist. But if he rejects the mode of
renewal proffered within the Christian solution as no longer
adequate to man's needs, it is to search, however obscurely,
for a more mysterious kind of renewal. What this is must await
our analysis of the myth's outworking, but it is necessary to
establish at this point the cruciality of the attempt Jeffers is
making, and to hold in mind that in the making, certain residual
Christian elements in his heritage, and hence in our own, are
powerfully in play.

For Barclay is for Jeffers a Promethean figure, and Prometheus is the figure that most centrally binds the two sides of
Jeffers' heritage and our own, the Greek and the Christian.
Small wonder, then, that Jeffers should encounter this archetype
very early in the working out of his creative destiny. It came
first to him in the ordeal of his *anima,* the feminine component
within himself. For Tamar too had been a Promethean figure,
the girl who crossed all the tribal taboos to fetch the fire of freedom and accepted consummation in that fire. But it was inevitable that he should pit the image of masculinity, his *animus**,
to the same attempt, and it is significant that for him this is the
image of the father.

Now to me it is apparent that, compared simply as figures,

---

* I depart in this instance from the practice of Jung for whom of course the word
animus is used to designate the masculine principle in women. "I must try," writes
D'Arcy in *The Mind and Heart of Love,* "to show how the notions of active and pas-
sive, egoism and self-sacrifice, classical and romantic, life and death, masculine and
feminine, animus and anima are the two constituents or factors which give the clue
to the working of nature, the self and the love of self for God."

Tamar has a great deal more appeal than Barclay, and as a creation is more humanly "successful"—closer to us, more intimate
of our own spirit. For the artist is always closer to his *anima*, the
motivating force of his creativity. But the solution of Barclay is
more crucial to us *as a people*, for it is the male, the father, who
must solve the problem inherent in the traditional patriarchy in
any contemporary crisis. In that solution it is of the essence of
the scenario that Barclay must fail, since the Christian myth
had established the cruciality of failure, but it is also of its
essence that he must eventually succeed. Barclay's failure is
everywhere evident: the poem has revulsed the majority of its
readers from the day it was published. Our task must be to
search out and lay bare the obscure and perplexing measure of
his success. In order to do that we must approach the underlying
archetype, and probe more deeply into the figure of Prometheus
himself.

IX

"Among all the gods of Greece," writes Kerényi, in his pene-
trating study of the Fire-bringer myth, "it is Prometheus who
stands in the most remarkable relation to mankind. He presents
a striking resemblance and a striking contrast to the Christian
Savior." Prometheus presents in its utmost cruciality the tension of man's situation as a conscious being, with intelligence
and will, in all its ambiguity in relation to the Absolute. In the
Christian tradition, therefore, it is not strange to find that the
figure of this god was appropriated as a prototype behind the
emergence of the Redeemer Himself. In *Lucifer and Prometheus* R.J. Zwi Werblowsky writes:

> No wonder, then, that in spite of the many profound differences be-
> tween the two myths, the early Fathers could point to Prometheus as
> the symbol of Christ. Tertullian speaks of the *crucibus Caucasorum*
> and exclaims: *Verus Prometheus, deus omnipotens, blasphemiis lan-*

cinatus, whilst others found god-and-man in a bold anagram *(Pro-theus)*, or dilated on the similarities of the sufferings of Prometheus and the passion of Christ, comparing Zeus' eagle to the lance, the Oceanides to the disciples, Cheiron's descent to Hades with that of Christ to hell, the virgin conception of Io and of Mary, and more fond similarities of this sort.

But this is not the way Prometheus began, for when he is first encountered in Hesiod he is an outright rebel and villain. It is not until Aeschylus five centuries later that we are confronted with the right-about-face that permits Prometheus to emerge as a hero and allows the Church Fathers to assimilate him to Christ. That this is possible is due to an inherent ambiguity in the archetype upon which the Promethean symbol is founded. Werblowsky summarizes:

> The Promethean myth thus betrays an interesting ambivalence, and shows itself capable of developing in two directions. As a typical Lucifer, "bringer of light", Prometheus shares the full ambivalence of this archetypal image. He has a light and a dark side, which can either differentiate into two sharply distinguished figures (as has happened with the original Lucifer) or else remains a multivalent, amorphous whole, lending itself, at the bid of occasion, to absorption by an amalgamation with other, more clear-cut and determined images. The Promethean myth can thus point towards Christ as well as towards Satan, according to our susceptibilities and our views about man, as imposed on us by our civilization and the exigencies of our psychic situation.

It is by virtue of this ambivalence that Thomas Merton, in preparing his own meditation on the mythical hero, discovers Erasmus in the sixteenth century reverting to the original Hesiodic version, and realizes that the Renaissance effected a profound reversal of attitude toward God by manipulating the symbol from its beneficent to its malignant aspects, with meaningful consequences for modern man:

> The two faces of Prometheus [he writes] represent two attitudes

toward life, one positive, the other negative. It is significant that the
Renaissance, in choosing between the two, selected the negative. It
is against this negative choice that my Prometheus is written. My
meditation is a rejection of the negative, modern myth of Prometheus. It is a return to the archaic, Aeschylean and positive aspect
of Prometheus, which is, at the same time, to my mind, deeply and
implicitly Christian. The Prometheus of Hesiod is Cain. The Prometheus of Aeschylus is Christ on the Cross.

It is true that in his meditation Merton does give us the
Christian version of Prometheus as it came down to us in the
great Catholic tradition, the archetype, one might say, fulfilled
by the great Age of Faith. But I feel that Merton oversimplifies
in attributing to modern man a Prometheus identified with
Cain, pure and simple. We will not be able to understand the
contemporary Promethean figure unless we recognize that
powerful Christian elements are retained in it. However, Merton has seen that the difference between the versions of Hesiod
and Aeschylus lies in the attitude toward the implacable father
figure, Zeus.

Hesiod represents and approves the Olympian order, where Zeus
reigns in absolute power over the subversive and dethroned gods of
archaic Greece. Zeus is the god of the invading Achaians who destroyed the matriarchal and tribal society of primitive Greece, the
society of the Earth Mother, of Demeter, of Hera and Athene. Prometheus, the son of Earth and of Ocean is a threat to the static order
established by Zeus, the order in which no bird may chirp and no
flower may look at the sun without the permission of the jealous Father. Zeus is the master of life rather than its giver. He tolerates man
and man's world, but only barely.

According to Hesiod, when Prometheus *stole* the fire for men (there
was no other way in which he could get fire away from Zeus) Zeus
revenged himself on Prometheus in the way we well know with the
added detail that he drives a stake through his heart. But Zeus is
also revenged upon mankind: how? By sending woman.

Strange, ponderous fantasy of an aggressively male society! Woman comes from Zeus as a *punishment*, for in her "everything is good but her heart."

Woman, the culminating penance in a life of labor and sorrow! . . .

But the five centuries that lay between Hesiod and the Greek tragedians brought a complete reversal in attitude toward the father, an attitude effected by a corresponding reversal in feeling toward woman:

> The Prometheus of Aeschylus is the exact opposite of the Prometheus of Hesiod. Between Prometheus and the Earth Mother and Ocean rises the figure of a usurper. For in Aeschylus it is Zeus, not Prometheus, who is the usurper. It is Zeus, not Prometheus, who is sick with hubris. True, Prometheus is driven by desperation beyond the wise limits which the Greek mind recognized so well. But his rebellion is the rebellion of life against inertia, of mercy and love against tyranny, of humanity against cruelty and arbitrary violence. And he calls upon the feminine, the wordless, the timelessly moving elements to witness his sufferings. Earth hears him.

Kerényi does not discuss the distinction between the Prometheus of Hesiod and that of Aeschylus, but he does recognize that the problem is more complex than Merton lets us know. In his view Prometheus, as we saw, "presents a striking resemblance *and a striking contrast* to the Christian Savior."

> More than any other Greek god, he intercedes for mankind, makes common cause with men. Therein lies the resemblance. But Christ suffered human existence as a man. His whole mission depended on his close bond with mankind. The paradox in his case is not that he, a man, made common cause with mankind. The paradox is the faith of the Christians who believe him to be a god.

It is apparent that Jeffers' rejection of the Christian paradox of Christ, the being who appeared to be a man and yet proved himself God, has thrown the Promethean archetype within his own psyche back upon the original tension in pre-Christian consciousness, and that in doing so he encountered the opposite face of Prometheus: Prometheus as Cain. But it could never be Cain, pure and simple. The Christ element in the symbol may be played down, but never extirpated. What this means is a terrible tension, an unbearable strain, in the symbol itself. And given the rupture of modern life that strain will intensify into madness. In the psychological shambles following World War I, Yeats's rough beast, its hour come round at last, slouching toward Bethlehem to be born, became for Jeffers the Rev. Dr. Barclay, climbing Pico Blanco for a new Mount Sinai.

X

That for Jeffers Barclay is a Promethean Cain rather than a Promethean Christ is signified straightaway by his insanity. But the madness is more than a symbol. It is also a device to brush aside the structure of conscious determination and localize the protagonist's motivation as a "private impurity". Too many cases of false prophets exist to deny it, but what interests us is the totality of Jeffers' rejection, his all-inclusive dismissal, tagging not only Barclay but every other religious prophet, even the greatest, with some fatal flaw. From the point of view of *Point Sur* the operative defect seems to be a consuming need for disciples. Since this is also a chief Jeffers contention against the historical Jesus, it becomes one of our clues to the fact that Barclay is actually a Christ-figure. Of more immediate concern is the reason. Why, one asks, is the cultivation of disciples an "impurity"?

It cannot be denied that Jeffers, in his answer, accords with a dominant school of contemporary psychology. Freud was not the first to assert it, but he certainly made such attributions popular. Coming from Jeffers that is precisely what makes us suspicious of it. The cultivation of disciples is seen as corrupt because it is founded on an unconscious evasion, a secret reflex toward personal power justified as an ultimate service, a purely substitutive device by which what was given and received as a blessing was actually an error, an evil, a curse. Jung himself, as we saw in his note on the "mana personality" delineated the inflational root of the malady, and warned of its universal threat to the charismatic man; but for him it was simply a dangerous phase, an unavoidable pitfall on an authentic quest. With Jeffers it is the totality of the attribution that disturbs us. For as an all-inclusive generality the clear position of the record is against it. Though unquestionably the monomyth does attest to the hero's ability to remain in the other world, the visionary realm above and beyond the common lot of life, nevertheless this is by no means the norm, but rather seems more in the nature of a privilege serving to emphasize to men the awesome completeness of a state infinitely superior to their own.

> The full round, the norm of the monomyth, requires that the hero shall now begin the labor of bringing the runes of wisdom, the Golden Fleece, or his sleeping princess, back into the kingdom of humanity, where the boon may redound to the renewing of the community, the nation, the planet, or the ten thousand worlds.

> But the responsibility has been frequently refused. Even the Buddha, after his triumph, doubted whether the message of realization could be communicated, and saints are reported to have passed away while in the supernal ecstasy. Numerous indeed are the heroes fabled to have taken up residence forever in the blessed isle of the unaging Goddess of Immortal Being.

That Jeffers would reject such "boons" as inflational in no way alters his essential agreement with the monomyth that the first step, the main step, is to break the grip of the mind on its own normative processes, cross the threshold —"cast one's humanity" as he says — and enter the interior freedom. His wish to remain there, fulfilled in his own version of the boon, is granted by the monomyth itself. What it does not grant him is his out-of-hand indictment of those who return. For the historic course, the "normal" course, demands the hero's re-entry into the everyday reality he left, and not by virtue of the Jeffersian attribution of the mana-personality, but by a deeper law intrinsic in the nature of contingent being itself. Campbell continues:

> Whether rescued from without, driven from within, or gently carried along by the guiding divinities, he has yet to re-enter with his boon the long-forgotten atmosphere where men who are fractions imagine themselves to be complete. He has yet to confront society with his ego-shattering, life-redeeming elixir, and take the return blow of reasonable queries, hard resentment, and good people at a loss to comprehend.

It is a confrontation which, of its very nature, constitutes a service, and as a service presupposes, for maximum effectiveness, the presence of disciples. It has always been so. Right into our own time Ouspensky, intent on the mystic way, questioning Gurdjieff's preoccupation with esoteric groups, got the Master's reply:

> The point is that a "group" is the beginning of everything. One man can do nothing, can attain nothing. A group with a real leader can do more. A group of people can do what one man can never do.

> You do not realize your own situation. You are in prison. All you can wish for, if you are a sensible man, is to escape. But how escape? It is necessary to tunnel under a wall. One man can do nothing. But let us suppose there are ten or twenty men —if they work in turn and if one covers another they can complete the tunnel and escape.

> Furthermore, no one can escape from prison without the help of those *who have escaped before*. Only they can say in what way escape is possible or can send tools, files, or whatever may be necessary. But *one* prisoner alone cannot find these people or get into touch with them. An organization is necessary. Nothing can be achieved without an organization.

With the evidence before us suddenly we are tempted to turn on Jeffers and demand of him an accounting. Why this agony about disciples? Is it Barclay or is it yourself, Jeffers, who is in trouble, immobilized by a really private impurity, a buried fear of love, a shame of your own tenderness, your own essential humanity — perhaps, actually, fear of that germ of homosexuality latent in every man which psychology has laid bare as the root of so much masculine hardness? And if so, is *Point Sur* a massive cover-up of your own demon, the intense pageantry behind which the hidden conflict is acted out, yet so contrived as to escape the vigilance of the bemused ego, only too glad to be reassured that the intensity of the drama is the guarantee of the purity of the motive?

The matter is important because if Jeffers' list of "intentions" means anything at all it indicates that more than any other of his long poems this one was "programmatic." *Point Sur* was written just as fame enveloped him, and we cannot but suspect that this poem is his most intense and apocalyptic because the nerve of something enormously seductive — the public man's almost feminine thirst for adulation — had been touched, a "private impurity" so tempting that he dare not acknowledge it, lest he succumb, and be consumed.

Jeffers, doubtless, would have his answers, and he is entitled to them. As a poet's answers we might expect them to have an elementary grounding in philosophy and science, but we will not receive them, to accept or reject, only in terms of that philosophy or that science. We will understand that the true answers of a poet are beyond him, visitational solutions emerging from the fabric of an inspired utterance, a synthesis of intuition from a world, a cognitive realm, which philosophy and science are unable to reach. Despite our glance at the man Jeffers himself, what we are attempting here is not so much to solve the problem of his motivation but to localize the nucleus out of which the poem emerged. That nucleus, that archetype, is certainly the Hero-Redeemer, the Promethean savior. But it

is revealed to us — and this is its cruciality for modern times —
not under its positive but under its negative aspects. We are
offered a redeemer who, on the conscious level, revolts us to the
basis of our being.

And yet, our revulsion is somehow gainsaid by the very
quality, the æsthetic tension, the indefinable force of the shat-
tering narrative of *Point Sur*. In recognizing this we are driven
to conclude that for Jeffers to generate such intensity, and the
specific kind of intensity this poem evinces, merely to delineate
a contemporary illusion, is difficult to believe. Whatever that
peculiar quality is, however we estimate it, and however we
respond to it, it is simply too oppressive, too compelling. It is
too "real" to be a mere device.

What that force suggests to me is that behind the passion
this poet is unconsciously creating, *through denial*, the positive, or efficacious aspect he ostensibly seeks to reject; that the
actual result, whatever his "intention," is truly to evoke from
the deeps of his negation an efficacious redeemer. Thus by
denying his hero any "truth," denying him even rationality, he
is enabled to press him forward through a processive stripping
away into a new order, an area of awareness never penetrated
to before. I say never penetrated to before because the findings
of astronomy and physics have disclosed a material cosmos
unconceived of in the history of man's thought, a cosmos that
seems to prophesy the absolute negation of man's racial ambition. Given this unprecedented cosmic prospect, what Jeffers
has done is put a typical prophet — a religious seeker bearing
all the psychic liabilities an accusative clinical psychology could
attribute to him — through a test run in order to determine if
any affirmation possibly survives the extremes of such negation, of such nihilism. It is my belief that Barclay's quintessen-
tial truth does just that.

XI

Mostly, however, these answers will yield only to a penetration into the fabric of the narrative itself, as seen in the poet's unconscious imagery, and in the implicit valuation of his diction. But as we pursue them we must make sure that we protect ourselves against the personalistic *cul de sac* that Jeffers himself succumbed to in his treatment of Jesus — I mean Jeffers' merely private fear of disciples. We must take into account the possibility that this revulsion may actually originate in something collective, may in some way be symptomatic of a condition within collective consciousness itself, and for the prophet to crave or accept disciples is now not only personalistically sick but racially perverse as well, a dangerous collective regression. If this is so the man of excessive charismatic potential must resolutely forbear appropriating to himself those reactionary elements which the recessive aspects of the collective unconscious only too eagerly thrust upon him. Campbell writes:

> The problem of mankind today, therefore, is precisely the opposite to that of men in the comparatively stable periods of those great co-ordinating mythologies which now are known as lies. Then all meaning was in the group, in the great anonymous forms, none in the self-expressive individual; today no meaning is in the group – none in the world: all is in the individual. But there the meaning is absolutely unconscious. One does not know toward what one moves. One does not know by what one is propelled. The lines of communication between the conscious and the unconscious zones of the human psyche have all been cut, and we have been split in two.

From this point of view it may well be that Jeffers, in the artist's heroic role as purifier of consciousness, by refusing the lure of disciples, by extirpating through Barclay the collective's now impure need for hero-redeemers, does truly fulfill his obligation to protect the race against its own regressions. In writing his book he fulfills his role as prophet; in refusing to found a movement or become a *guru* he forces the collective to grope forward beyond any premature fixation upon human intermediaries. No self-gratifying egoism must permit it to deflect from its destiny, its own naked encounter with the naked God.

XII

But the time has come for us to put aside speculation and enter the work itself. Beginning with the Prologue as a sort of weathering process, we can expect it to furnish the conditioning interval we need for our acclimatization, orient us into the prospective violence, and at the same time protect us from psychic inundation by too direct an exposure to the blast of action itself. If it is to do this it must be forceful, evocative and intense, and must seize us with the Giant Hand that is the true signature of genius. For as Erich Neumann writes:

> Every transformative or creative process comprises stages of possession. To be moved, captivated, spellbound, signify to be possessed by something; and without such a fascination and the emotional tension connected with it, no concentration, no lasting interest, no creative process, are possible. Every possession can justifiably be interpreted either as a one-sided narrowing or as an intensification and deepening. The exclusivity and radicality of such "possession" represent both an opportunity and a danger. But no great achievement is possible if one does not accept this risk . . .

It is in his magnificent Prelude that Jeffers first possesses us, prepares us to "accept the risk," forces us into the mythological dimension where all the violations may be endured without flinching, and where we may grope forward toward whatever solutions we can find to the ritual of deliverance and ordeal which constitutes the opportunity or the destruction of modern man.

It is one of the masterpieces of Jeffers' art, exhibiting to maximum degree his complex technical skills. And it reveals much about the questions the poem proposes, and some intimation of their answers. I was long of the opinion that it was created well after the inception of the narrative itself. A poet will enter into a theme tentatively, not fully engaged, expecting to deepen his involvement as he goes. Then, finally committed, he turns back and strokes in his opening, able at last to operate somewhere near the level of his subsistent æsthetic commitment. Indeed, the shift in psychic tension between the Prelude and the first section seemed evidence enough that this was the case. But when I examined the Jeffers papers in the Yale Collection of American Literature I saw it was not so. The poet wrote the Prelude as we have it and proceeded immediately to the narrative. Thus we see that it is indeed the psychological matrix out of which the whole work develops. More important, it is the "door," the threshold over which we must pass in order to effect a shift in attitude from our normative consciousness, in order to leave the world of "actuality" and enter the world of "myth."

This, the world of myth, is the dimension into which the Prologue takes us, and it does so masterfully. Beautiful, intense, vibrant with urgency, flecked with lightning flashes of scorn and repudiation, it hovers over our world like the entry of one of the great storms which it invokes above the Carmel coast, and introduces us not only to the climate of mind and the figures we are going to encounter, but also to the basic religious symbols that lie in all their primitiveness beneath our culture. It creates the psychic atmosphere which evokes the presence of the "deliverer," the man Barclay himself.

*

The Prelude opens powerfully:

> *I drew solitude over me, on the lone shore,*
> *By the hawk-perch stones; the hawks and the gulls are never*
>   *breakers of solitude.*

And savagely:

> *When the animals Christ was rumored to have died for drew in,*
> *The land thickening, drew in about me, I planted trees eastward,*
> *   and the ocean*
> *Secured the west with the quietness of thunder. I was quiet.*

And contemptuously:

> *Imagination, the traitor of the mind, has taken my solitude and*
> *   slain it.*
> *No peace but many companions; the hateful-eyed*
> *And human-bodied are all about me: you that love multitude may*
> *   have them.*

It would seem Jeffers is saying that though he prefers solitude
and has taken steps to ensure it, the invasion of Carmel in the
twenties shifted the psychic balance the region had provided
him and overbalanced the soul with the fervid restlessness of
the normative American mentality: gregarious, talkative, slap-
happy, trivial, mundane, unreflective — all polar opposites to
the quietude of the elements. More likely at a far deeper level
he is saying that Fame, which has in fact come to him, has
touched some somnolent nerve of response, and he must either
accept its stimulus and succumb to it, or utterly reject its appeal.

At any rate he has scoffed at our values, and in scoffing in-
trigued us with the power of the negative. Yet the negative must
be uttered, and utterance is positive. He proclaims himself vulnerable.

> *But why should I make fables again? There are many*
> *Tellers of tales to delight women and the people.*
> *I have no vocation.*

The power of the depth throws him back upon the underlying
awareness of permanence and stability:

> *   The old rock under the house, the hills with their*
> *   hard roots and the ocean hearted*
> *With sacred quietness from here to Asia.*

But he cannot rest there, despite himself he is driven to engage
in what he despises:

> *Make me ashamed to speak of the active little bodies, the coupling*
> *   bodies, the misty brainfuls*
> *Of perplexed passion.*

Against the immense impersonal gravity and masculine permanence of things, it is this itch, the female sexual itch, that
confronts him. Why?

Why not? Carmel, the summer cottages and love-nests of
the Jazz Age, week-ending business men with their hot mam-
mas, drunk on green liquor smuggled in by boat from Canada.
Carmel, where Aimee Semple McPherson, the torrid evangelist
from Southern California, would hole up with her paramour
while the nation scoured the byways enthusiastically search-
ing for her kidnapped person.

> *   Humanity is needless.*
> *I said, "Humanity is the start of the race, the gate to break away*
> *   from, the coal to kindle,*
> *The blind mask crying to be slit with eye-holes."*

That was in "The Tower Beyond Tragedy," a flashback into
Aeschylus's world, when civilization as we know it was just
beginning.

> *Well, now it is done, the mask slit, the rag burnt, the starting-post*
> *   left behind: but not in a fable.*

What was then projected as a prophecy has become in actuality
a hard fact:

> *Culture's outlived, art's root-cut, discovery's*
> *The way to walk in.*

The poet's duty is no longer to seek ways to prefigure what will
be, but to scrawl it out crudely and be done:

> *   Only remains to invent the language to tell it.*
> *   Match-ends of burnt experience*
> *Human enough to be understood,*
> *Scraps and metaphors will serve.*

For if the race has burnt itself out, then only burnt out images
are necessary to show it to itself. The time when Christ must
speak in parables because the people were incapable of appre-
hending is over. Jeffers reaches for the heart of the parable to
show actuality to a post-Christian people:

> *The wine was a little too strong for the new wine-skins.*

It is important here not to be stung into feeling insulted, into
contemptuous dismissal. We are overhearing a man in dialogue
with himself. We share, in some measure, his difficulties. Profoundly religious, he loves solitude and permanence, and he
seeks out the symbols and images that confirm these truths to
himself. But he is shaken, too, with excesses, the fretful and
itching acerbations of imagination and dissolution. He has seen
those realities increase as the culture proliferated, until by the
mid-twenties of this century they were at boiling point. He
longs for silence but he is impelled to speak. He despises speaking but speak he must. "The active little bodies, the coupling
bodies, the misty brainfuls of perplexed passion." He projects
them outside himself, but they are his own projections, and he
cannot escape them. For him, a poet, there is only one solution,
and that is the creative act. Drawing down within himself,
against the stagnation of his conscious mind where the tension
has been equalized because the forces countercheck each other,
he calls up the great image of creative release, the great archetypal centrality that dominates the Prelude.

> Come storm, kind storm.
> *Summer and the days of tired gold*
> *And bitter blue are more ruinous.*
> *The leprous grass, the sick forest.*
> *The sea like a whore's eyes,*
> *And the noise of the sun,*
> *The yellow dog barking in the blue pasture,*
> *Snapping sidewise.*

What then is needed? To restore the roots of viability beneath
the sterility of corrupt culture. Zimmer says:

> Ages and attitudes of man that are long gone by still survive in the
> deeper unconscious layers of our soul. The spiritual heritage of ar-
> chaic man (the ritual and mythology that once visibly guided his
> conscious life) has vanished to a large extent from the surface of the
> tangible and conscious realm, yet survives and remains ever present
> in the subterranean layers of the unconscious. It is the part of our be-
> ing that links us to a remote ancestry and constitutes our involunatry
> kinship with archaic man and with ancient civilizations and tradi-
> tions.

It is the sovereign role of the poet to perform this function for
modern man. If the politician appropriates that role and perverts it for the uses of power, creating a fascism which by appeal to blood and soil perverts the needs of the people to be
restored to their roots, he pre-empts but does not invalidate the
office of the poet. Hitler does not invalidate Wagner. Jeffers
despised fascism, but he did not permit its misappropriations to
deter him from his archetypal function as source-seeker for the
race.

Now the summer stagnation, image of our rationally dominated culture, in the extremity of its drought, invokes its
redeemer, the "kind storm." It is the image of renewal in the
creative act, the Dionysian syndrome, and it holds its terrific
potential of deliverance: one of those great storms that form on
the upper Pacific and start southward bringing winds, rains, and
the violence of lightning. This violence is seen as non-human
and divine, and it has its correspondence in the human soul:

> When I remembered old rains,
> Running clouds and the iron wind, then the trees trembled.
> I was calling one of the great dancers
> Who wander down from the Aleutian rocks and the open Pacific,
> Pivoting counter-sunwise, celebrating power with the whirl of a
> dance, sloping to the mainland.

I watched his feet waken the water
And the ocean break in foam beyond Lobos;
The iron wind struck from the hills.

This noble and sublime titanic center of energy serves us as prototype to the figure of Barclay himself — not as a "personification of natural force," for clearly here the storm itself is characterized as an archetypal figure. But the conventionalized rational structure of materialistic civilization is heavily established and refuses to yield.

You are tired and corrupt,
You kept the beast under till the fountain's poisoned,
He drips with mange and stinks through the oubliette window.

Here we are introduced to the underlying psychological apparatus of the poem. The oubliette, a dungeon with an opening only at the top, is a crude symbol of the Freudian version of the unconscious. If the instincts, the "beast," are repressed too long, they will corrupt the conscious powers themselves. Even the recent bloodbath of World War I did not slake or heal these tendencies, for the slaughter was so great that those who might have come back appeased, and hence given balance to society, were themselves killed off, leaving the survivors no better than before:

The promise-breaker war killed whom it freed,
And none living's the cleaner.

But the creative potential remains:

Yet storm comes, the lions hunt
In the nights striped with lightning. It will come: feed on peace
While the crust holds.

He warns the complacent, in a fatherly tone:

to each of you at length a little
Desolation; a pinch of lust or a drop of terror.

And we make our exit from the areas of rational disquisition as the images fade and blend together in the cadences of appease-

ment and release, a falling asleep or a drift into Dionysian deliverance:

> Then the lions hunt in the brain of the dying: storm is good, storm
>   is good, good creature,
> Kind violence, throbbing throat aches with pity.

Now we are introduced to one of the principal figures of the
drama, Onorio Vasquez, who stands between two worlds, the
practical and the visionary. Of all the characters in the drama,
only he survives to appear in other Jeffers narratives. He is
watching his brothers crucify a hawk, the principal symbol for
Jeffers of divinity in act, and by virtue of this crucifixion, is
identified with Christ, an identification made earlier by Hopkins in his "Windhover," though it is problematical whether
at that time Jeffers had seen that poem — more likely it is an
instance of an underlying archetype precipitating an identical
insight in two widely separated poets.

> They crucified the creature,
> A nail in the broken wing on the barn wall
> Between the pink splinters of bone and a nail in the other.
> They prod his breast with a wand, no sponge of vinegar,
> "Fly down, Jew-beak."

The hawk, the Christ-like male symbol, introduces Onorio's
prophetic mind to its feminine counterpart, a figure corresponding in archetypal dimension to the storm, the great dancer
that had preceded her on the water. In the galley proofs of the
poem at Yale certain details of her sketch were excised due,
according to a note affixed to the portfolio, to the censorship
situation at that time. I give the passage, with the kind permission of the curators at Yale, as it exists in the galley proofs.

> What he sees:
> The ocean like sleek gray stone perfectly jointed
> To the heads and bays, a woman walking upon it,
> The curling scud of the storm around her ankles,

Naked and strong, her thighs the height of the mountain, walking
  and weeping,
The shadow of hair under the belly, the jutting breasts like hills, the
  face in the hands and the hair
Streaming north.

Now the Christ-hawk identity is deepened. In the mind of
Onorio the archetypal woman on the sea is associated with the
mother of Jesus:

  "Why are you sad, our lady?" " I had only one son.
The strange lover never breaks the window-latches again
When Joseph's at synagogue."

Here the poet accommodates to the modernist interpretation of
the miracle of Mary's overshadowing by the Holy Spirit but
retains the necessary ambiguity, as the figure "strange lover"
fittingly retains the orthodox meaning as well. These ambiguities deepen the Christ-hawk visage into an almost Blakean
image of austere divinity:

  Orange eyes, tired and fierce,
They're casting knives at you now, but clumsily, the knives
Quiver in the wood, stern eyes the storm deepens.
Don't wince, topaz eyes.

Old Vasquez and his boys burn the mountain: fire, the symbol
of consuming fulfillment, of punishment and purgation. This
symbol takes us from the archetypal woman to the young wife
who yearns for erotic fulfillment but is frustrate, unable to
transmute her need into charismatic encounter, latching the
windows but forgetting the door:

  Myrtle Cartwright
Could sleep if her heart would quit moving the bed-clothes.

This heart-movement introduces Faith Heriot, seen here as a
pubescent girl, one of the main figures in the drama to come.
She lies to her father, who keeps, not Point Sur but Point Pinos
light, to get out in the dark. At last alone she lies under the

swinging light of the beacon, another phallic symbol of the restless energizing Spirit, rich with fertility images:

> *This girl never goes near the cowshed but wanders*
> *Into the dunes, the long beam of the light*
> *Swims over and over her head in the high darkness,*
> *The spray of the storm strains through the beam but Faith*
> *Crouches out of the wind in a hollow of the sand*
> *And hears the sea, she rolls on her back in the clear sand*
> *Shuddering, and feels the light lie thwart her hot body*
> *And the sand trickle into the burning places.*

We have before this been given the suggestion of the dominant motif, that of strain, but now it rises to an incantatory chant, a function it will maintain throughout the poem:

> *Oh crucified*
> *Wings, orange eyes, open?*
> *Always the strain, the straining flesh, who feels what God feels*
> *Knows the straining flesh, the aching desires,*
> *The enormous water straining its bounds, the electric*
> *Strain in the cloud, the strain of the oil in the oil tanks*
> *At Monterey, aching to burn, the strain of the spinning*
> *Demons that make an atom, straining to fly asunder,*
> *Straining to rest at the center,*
> *The strain in the skull, blind strains, force and counterforce,*
> *Nothing prevails.*

Now we are at the heart of the psychic drama that centers the poem. We have entered the mythological dimension in which the poet is establishing himself: the opposed polarities of an aching mankind and aching Nature, an aching cosmos. Nothing can resolve this tension but release, and such are the opposed forces that release means violence—release means the consummation of the lesser element in the greater, a burnt out filament in a light bulb, Barclay burnt out at the mouth of the Womb-Tomb to end the drama: "Match-ends of burnt experience [just] Human enough to be understood." The end of the affair.

Now wind rises, introducing another aspect of Spirit (hawk, lover, lightning, wind):

> At Vasquez' place in the yellow
> Pallor of dawn the roof of the barn's lifting, his sons cast ropes
>   over the timbers. The crucified
> Snaps his beak at them. He flies on two nails.
> Great eyes, lived all night?
> Onorio should have held the rope but it slid through his fingers.
>   Onorio Vasquez
> Never sees anything to the point. What he sees:
> The planted eucalyptuses bent double
> All in a row, praying north, "Why everything's praying
> And running northward, old hawk anchored with nails
> You see that everything goes north like a river.
> On a cliff in the north
> Stands the strange lover, shines and calls."

The great phallic lighthouse joins the litany of energy-forces assimilated to Spirit.

> Myrtle Cartwright in the seep of dawn can abide no longer.

Her husband is away. She starts through the storm to find her lover. When she flees to her profane lover the lightning as symbol of Spirit overtakes her and covers her like a beast. But it is not a beast:

> The lightnings like white doves hovering her head harmless as
>   pigeons, through great bars of black music.
> She lifts her wet arms. "Come, doves."

The dove was employed as an erotic symbol centuries before Christian iconography applied it to the Holy Spirit. This overshadowing, this conception, was occasioned by the igniting of the oil tanks by lightning in Monterey. As the atoms split and explode the release from the strain is granted in marriage, the symbols of sexual consummation:

> The oil tank boils with joy in the north . . .
> roars with fulfilled desire,

The ring-bound molecules splitting, the atoms dancing apart,
*   marrying the air.*

It all builds up to humanity's immolation in the forces behind itself. Human ache of desire will find its consummation, whether as did Myrtle Cartwright, who latched her window against the Spirit but left her door open to the world, or Onorio Vasquez, who longs to immolate his consciousness in a consummation greater than mankind's:

> *Don't you see any vision, Onorio Vasquez? "No, for the topazes*
> *Have dulled out of his head, he soars on two nails,*
> *Dead hawk over the coast. Oh little brother*
> *Julio, if you could drive nails through my hands*
> *I'd stand against the door: through the middle of the palms:*
> *And take the hawk's place, you could throw knives at me.*
> *I'd give you my saddle and the big bridle, Julio,*
> *With the bit that rings and rings when the horse twirls it."*
> *He smiles. "You'd see the lights flicker in my hair."*
> *He smiles craftily. "You'd live long and be rich,*
> *And nobody could beat you in running or riding."*
> *He chatters his teeth. "It is necessary for someone to be fastened*
> *   with nails.*
> *And Jew-beak died in the night. Jew-beak is dead."*

Thus ends the Prologue. The turning of the storm, the anguish of human desire, the promise of release in physical consummation, all have combined to take us out of our normative consciousness. The archetypal symbols unfold within us in their pristine originality and primitive vigor. We are given to understand that we are not to conceive of this narrative as a sequential account of human events, the drama of the heroic consciousness confronted with nature, or God, or itself. We are instead in the domain of collective myth, and "the myth disregards — does not even know — the individual." Projections of subsistent human consciousness are called up from the deeps and extended into the cruciality of engagement with the cosmos and the spirit. They are given names but they are not to be seen as personalities. Neither are they "coagulations of human plexi." They are personifications of the elements of man's inner being which have lost contact with one another and have started forward each on its own path of deliverance.

Thus the solution posited in the possibility of humanity's having passed beyond the need for a redeemer is, as the saying goes, "up for grabs." Everything about these personifications indicates that they are ripe for a deliverer, a true hero, a true superman, who is of the essence of mythical awareness, and who must needs arise if the separating consciousnesses are to be held together. "It is necessary for someone to be fastened with nails." In the debased religiosity and cultural vitiation of the Jazz Age, its triviality, its itching and squirming libido, its profane ignorance and its corrosive cynicism, the anthropocentric version of the God of Christianity will not avail. "Jew-beak is dead." Instead emerges a new hero, a new messiah, a new superman. He will seek to weld all together in a terrible act of unbelievable affirmation — an affirmation beyond the limits of common human desire, beyond common hope. He will free himself through the ancient acts of violation — fornication, incest, rape — and he will carry his followers to the mouth of the tomb. His name is fated to eat like acid, to become a stumbling block to the perplexed literate intelligence of his time. His name is The Rev. Dr. Arthur Barclay, and he is headed for Point Sur. It remains to be seen whether his creator will realize or deny the hunger that gave him birth.

XIII

And so, having touched some of the strands of motif and implication that might help us on our way, having immersed ourselves in the compulsive atmosphere of storm, dissolution and renewal that so powerfully pervades the Prelude, we stand at last on the lip of the initiating action, and face forward into the consequential dimension of the myth itself. In treating of the Prelude we have seen the present condition of human collectiveness delineated, its alienation from God and nature, its need of a redeemer to take it back into contact with the making forces of reality, sources of renewal long repressed under metallic surfaces. We have seen, too, something of the individual dimension, the personal adventure posited as initiation rite. A society without religious orientation in depth cries out for a messiah to take it back to its origins. But it cannot produce such a messiah for it has lost the spiritual attitude that makes it possible for him to emerge, and it has jettisoned the techniques that might enable him to perfect himself, be sufficient to the task that would confront him.

Thus it is possible to see in *Point Sur* the two tendencies, the collective and the individual, on a "collision course," and we might read the unfolding of its scenario with that in mind. As the various personifications typified by the cast of characters emerge — Natalia Morhead, Faith Heriot, Maruca, Randal — their essential rootlessness and inversion signify that they are cut off from centrality, and hence must react like loose flotsam, or metallic particles. Barclay, on the other hand, possessed by the collectivity's need for a messiah, is unable to withstand its compelling demand. It is a demand so overpowering that only the most perfectly formed consciousness could fulfill it, a consciousness which, paradoxically, the collectivity has renounced the capacity to produce. Thus, as it reacts to his presence and becomes more and more intense around him, Barclay himself burns with a more single intensity toward destruction. We are justified, then, in seeing the dénouement at Point Sur as the crisis of a culture, a culture cut off at the roots and delivered to the consequence of its spiritual ignorance.

But, it must be insisted, this is not the position of Jeffers himself. He is registering not the crisis of a culture but the crisis of mankind. For him the more "whole" traditional sacral cultures of the past were no better, essentially, than the painfully rootless ones of today. Why? Because science has shown their beliefs to be as illusionary as ours. The cosmos of Jeffers is essentially a Newtonian one. The religious transposition made available through the shift from Newtonian to Einsteinian physics came too late for him. Nineteenth-century science had demolished the Christian God as an anthropomorphism, and explained religion, no matter what its substance, as mere compensation. The process by which sacral man had staved off disintegration, forms of ritual and meditation sufficient to balance the collective consciousness and produce messiahs in times of crisis — these were, one and all, provisional solutions, efficacious only within the pathetic limits of human consciousness, while those who rose to the bait — Christ, Gautama, Lao Tze— did so out of private impurity. In *Point Sur* Jeffers is putting that solution through its final test-run. He is doing it in order to demonstrate that it will no longer do, has in fact, never done. In "Theory of Truth" he asks over, as we saw, the questions Barclay has asked. Sketching the private impurity of the three great prophets he asks again:

> *Then search for truth*
> *is foredoomed and frustrate?*
> *Only stained fragments?*

And answers:

> *Until the mind has turned its love*
> *from itself and man, from parts to the whole.*

XIV

And yet, even as he utters it, he gives the game away. Even for himself, this solution never sufficed. I am not speaking in terms of the inadequacy of his philosophy; I am speaking in terms of the problem posited by his creative drive. *Point Sur* moves out of the conditions of fragmented and isolated tension we saw in the Prelude and takes its course through a series of inter-reacting exchanges to final crystallization and utter annihilation at the point of conclusion. And whatever the philosophy is saying, the poetry is saying that this is good. All Jeffers' explanations, all his "intentions," do not ring true because they are all belied by the exultation of his verse.

How can this be? The essential attraction-revulsion syndrome upon which the ambivalence is poised is endemic to human nature. But it is so strong in Jeffers that he is willing to intensify contingency in order to clinch it. This is the fact. It could never, for him, suffice to "turn from man," turn "from the parts to the whole." Because to turn, to see, is itself to manifest contingency, and contingency is excruciating. What is the One and what are the Many? To crystallize consciousness in participation in the whole is Jeffers' consuming need, the existence of his verse attests to it. He declares the opposite. He proclaims the necessity, and his willingness, to achieve a life of ego-annulling contemplation. His poetics deny it. Intense, passionate, onrushing, needful and aching, his volcanic rhythms intensify contingency rather than annul it. Yet, somehow, through that crystallized contingency he touches finality, the living glimpse of annihilation. Annihilation. "The most beautiful word." And how are we to conceive of annihilation? It is, essentially, unspeakable; but in a thousand contingent images he evokes it metaphorically. The night. The peace. The quietude. The timelessness. Over and over he creates the images of contingency in order to indicate the substance of his need, which is to pass beyond what he has created, what he has seen, what he has desired.

And in fact the whole effort and achievement of his poem is to establish the ordeal, transmute its agonies into transcendence, and pass beyond transcendence into — what? Well, actually, beatitude. But beatitude as seen from the point of the utter negative. From the positive point of view, beatitude would be the Beatific Vision of the Christian, or the Nirvana of the Buddhist, but Jeffers fights shy of either. They are too conceptual for him. He is aware of the over-mastering presence of God, but the liability of his basic contingency makes him contemptuous of accepting any kind of beatitude based on any kind of deduction from the Reality he has sought.

I suppose his essential role as poet prevents him, actually, from settling for the eventualities of either the philosopher, the seer, or the mystic. Jeffers as poet can only *create* the condition of his beatitude, and when he calls it Annihilation he is thinking of the cancelling *in itself* of that appetitive need within him which is the æsthetic impulse and whose mode is the creative act. So he creates his death, severally, and over and over, in his various narratives and descriptive poems.

In *Tamar* he cast the first spear. He took the *anima*, the feminine principle in himself, and drove it to the point of annihilation, consumed in the fires of the House of Incest. She would not stay dead. In "Apology For Bad Dreams" she haunts him into telling how he encountered her, and years later in a poem called "Come Little Birds" that story is spelled out in detail. "I am Tamar Cauldwell. Tell them I had my desire." Next he took the *animus*, the masculine principle, and drove it to the point of annihilation. This is Barclay. But neither would the *animus* stay dead. In subsequent narratives he contented himself with exploring the ratios of inter-dependent contingencies and these are more contained, more formally resolved æsthetic structures, and are better liked. But he did not pitch the spear at the absolute again until "At the Birth of an Age" when, in the figure of Gudrun, he cast the *anima* once more. Gudrun does not burn with the same intenseness of naked potentiality that Tamar did; it was as if by that time Jeffers *knew* beforehand, whereas Tamar for him had been pure discovery, as Barclay was pure discovery. But nevertheless in the poem's closing pages the voice of the Nordic Gudrun merges with that of the Oriental Jesus to make a *heiros gamos*, a *conjunctio*, which together are subsumed into that of the Promethean Hanged God, the pure archetype of self-sustaining immolation, which is actually the voice of Barclay purged of its insanity and burning with unspeakable purity, the principle of subsistent consciousness upon which the whole of reality turns and sustains, the principle that Christians themselves perceive as the keynote of all being, and call the Christ:

> *If I were quiet and emptied myself of pain,*
> *breaking these bonds,*
> *Healing these wounds: without strain there is nothing. Without*
> *pressure, without conditions, without pain,*
> *Is peace; that's nothing, not-being; the pure night, the perfect*
> *freedom, the black crystal. I have chosen*
> *Being; therefore wounds, bonds, limits and pain; the crowded mind*
> *and the anguished nerves, experience and ecstasy.*
> *Whatever electron or atom or flesh or star or universe cries to me,*
> *Or endures in shut silence: it is my cry, my silence; I am the nerve,*
> *I am the agony,*
> *I am the endurance. I torture myself*
> *To discover myself; trying with a little or extreme experiment each*
> *nerve and fibril, all forms*
> *Of being, of life, of cold substance; all motions and netted*
> *complications of event,*
> *All poisons of desire, love, hatred, joy, partial peace, partial vision.*
> *Discovery is deep and endless,*
> *Each moment of being is new: therefore I still refrain my burning*
> *thirst from the crystal-black*
> *Water of an end.*

So we are not to see *Point Sur* as anything conclusive. We are lence in an attempt at transcendence. Before the cast was begun to see it as a try, a far-cast spear, thrown out of painful ambiva-

the understanding of what transcendence really consisted of was deeply forming in the underlying consciousness, but not articulated. *Tamar* had only glimpsed it. True, "Tower Beyond Tragedy" had posited the alternative of contemplation, but the archetypes of imbalance in Jeffer's nature were too acute to accept that. In *Point Sur* he tossed again, the longest, hardest, most intense cast of the spear he was ever to make, and he "touched his answer"—annihilation— the only answer that would ever appease *his* spirit. But he could not keep with it. The secondary calls of contemplation kept positing their claims, and he wrote out his remaining narratives (save one,"The Birth of an Age") to accommodate his needs, rather than discover them.

Now he possesses his answers. His spirit lives on in the annihilative center of the body of poems which constitute his work, the still center of the æsthetic intuition, whose term is beyond mediation, beyond subject and object, beyond contingency, beyond the subsidiary distinctions to the supreme Isness, where all things are annihilated within the abyss of Being, which he, and I, and all men, in our own way and by our own terms, have always called God. "But think on the nothing/Outside the stars," cried Barclay at the last, "the other shore of me, there's peace."

> He ran northward, his followers
> Tired and fell off. He alone, like a burnt pillar
> Smeared with the blood of sacrifice passed across the black hills,
> And then the gray ones, the fire had stopped at a valley.
> He came to a road and followed it, the waste vitality
> Would not be spent. When the sun stood westward he turned
> Away from the light and entered Mal Paso Canyon.
> At the head of the steep cleft men had mined coal
> Half a century before; acres of dry thistles
> Covered the place where men had labored, and Barclay
> Lay down in the mouth of the black pit. After three days,

Having not tasted water, he was dying and he said:
"I want creation . . ."

And so the tossed spear has turned in midair and is winging back to life. The ritual of initiation into death has been successful. It is an initiation into renewal. The mythological teleology is preserved, contained in the impenetrable diastole and systole that make up reality. Annihilation is only the entry into the abyss of renewal. Barclay's heroic ordeal, crippled by unpreparedness, propelled by a collective need greater than he could withstand, was not in vain. In the deep psyche of the reader, violation after violation have been passed through, hell-hole after hell-hole penetrated and passed beyond. In death the old life is liberated into the new, and God speaks out of the throat of his mouthpiece:

"I want creation. The wind over the desert
Has turned and I will build again all that's gone down.
I am inexhaustible."

7

The Poet is Dead

A memorial for Robinson Jeffers, written
for The San Francisco Poetry Festival of 1962,
and reprinted, with a Note, from the limited
edition of the Auerhahn Press, 1964.

To Lawrence Clark Powell

I did not think it possible for me to write a commissioned poem of any kind, on any subject. When James Schevill asked various poets to do pieces for a projected Poetry Festival to be held at the San Francisco Museum of Art late in June of 1962 I accepted, knowing a poem would surely emerge in the interim which, truthfully enough, I could present as my offering. That was December, 1961. In January Jeffers died, and I did a tribute for *The Critic*, the Chicago review, concluding it by remarking that in acknowledging my early discipleship to him, a man I had never met because he had no use for disciples, I had at last, thanks to this opportunity, "paid my birth dues." It seemed as much as I could do. When Schevill urged me to make my Festival contribution a poem honoring Jeffers I demurred. As I say, I really did not think it possible for me to write a commissioned poem of any kind, on any subject.

What happened to make the elegy emerge, "move out of the possible and into the actual," and be ready for the Festival in June, I do not know, but it became apparent that my tribute in *The Critic* had not even scratched the surface. Now in the process of its emergence the poem made its own lordly and masterful way. It reached into those alluvial deposits of imagery that lay deep in my memory and brought up dominant Jeffersian figures for its use: The Bed by the Window, from the poem by that name; The Woman Called Life, from "To Death"; The Wolf Who Died Snapping, from "The Deer Lay Down Their Bones"; and of course that strange disturbing image from "Post Mortem" in which the exuberant women of the future, threatening the very fixtures of the poet's world, will "drink joy" from men's loins. Not only that but it rejected my attempt to write a poem receiving him into the Christian Afterlife — a belief which he had abandoned, I could only suppose, simply because he had not really understood. Instead, out of deference to his unshakable integrity, it compelled me to write my only poem *not* composed on a specifically Christian theme since my conversion twelve years before.

Or perhaps the incorporation of such direct figures from Jeffers' work into the poem was my need to bury, once and for all, those elements of my own past with him. Or again some might say that my inability to localize his figure in the Christian Afterlife really represents my failure to resolve the problem he posed for me — an interpretation I do not find threatening because I know that so much of what we are will be clarified only in that Afterlife itself.

Be that as it may, when the Festival came at last I stood up on the final night and read it heart and soul. The strophes seemed to find their subsistent disposition, their stone-like pace. They seemed to rise out of the substance of utterance itself, almost out of pure voice. Standing among them, surrounded by them, I, their author and receiver, saw with wonder that this must be because the actual vehicle of communication was the silence that set them apart. I saw that those silences were speaking louder than sound, my sound, ever could.

They spoke so loud some people were disturbed. The Book Editor of the *San Francisco Chronicle* reported that he had come for a "festival" and protested the preoccupation with death. But on stage I was unaware of that. I was with the silences, which for all their softness must have been speaking harder than I could tell.

If they did speak hard it was for the dead, and I wanted them to, no denying that. But I wanted them to speak even harder for the living, for me. I wanted them to say all the things for which I would never be able to find the words.

Kentfield, California
Kentfield Priory
November 7, 1963

To be read with a full stop between the strophes as in a dirge.

In the evening the dusk
    Stipples with lights. The long shore
    Gathers darkness in on itself
And goes cold. From the lap of silence
All the tide-crest's pivotal immensity
Lifts into the land.

The great tongue is dried.
The teeth that bit to the bitterness
Are sheathed in truth.

For the poet is dead.
The pen, splintered on the sheer
Excesses of vision, unfingered, falls.
The heart-crookt hand, cold as a stone,
Lets it go down.

If you listen
You can hear the field mice
Kick little spurts in the grasses.
You can hear
Time take back its own.

For the poet is dead.
On the bed by the window,
Where dislike and desire
Killed each other in the crystalline interest,
What remains alone lets go of its light. It has found
Finalness. It has touched what it craved: the passionate
Darks of deliverance.

At sundown the sea wind,
Burgeoning,
Bled the west empty.

Now the opulent
Treacherous woman called Life
Forsakes her claim. Blond and a harlot
She once drank joy from his narrow loins.
She broke his virtue in her knees.

In the water-gnawn coves of Point Lobos
The white-faced sea otters
Fold their paws on their velvet breasts
And list waveward.

But he healed his pain on the wisdom of stone,
He touched roots for his peace.

The old ocean boils its wrack,
It steeps its lees.

For the poet is dead. The gaunt wolf
Crawled out to the edge and died snapping.
He said he would. The wolf
Who lost his mate. He said he would carry the wound,
The blood-wound of life, to the broken edge
And die grinning.

Over the salt marsh the killdeer,
Unrestrainable,
Cry fear against moon set.

And all the hardly suspected
Latencies of disintegration
Inch forward. The skin
Flakes loss. On the death-gripped feet
The toenails glint like eyeteeth
From the pinched flesh.

The caged ribs and the bladed shoulders,
Ancient slopes of containment,
Imperceptibly define the shelves of structure,
Faced like rock ridges
Boned out of mountains, absently revealed
With the going of the snow.

In the sleeve of darkness the gopher
Tunnels the sod for short grass
And pockets his fill.

And the great phallus shrinks in the groin,
The seed in the scrotum
Chills.

When the dawn comes in again,
Thoughtlessly,
The sea birds will mew by the window.

For the poet is dead. Beyond the courtyard
The ocean at full tide hunches its bulk.
Groping among the out-thrusts of granite
It moans and whimpers. In the phosphorescent
Restlessness it chunks deceptively,
Wagging its torn appendages, dipping and rinsing
Its ripped sea rags, its strip-weeded kelp.
The old mother grieves her deathling.
She trundles the dark for her lost child.
She hunts her son.

On the top of the tower
The hawk will not perch tomorrow.

But in the gorged rivermouth

Already the steelhead fight for entry.
They feel fresh water
Sting through the sieves of their salt-coarsened gills.
They shudder and thrust.

So the sea broods. And the aged gull,
Asleep on the water, too stiff to feed,
Spins in a side-rip crossing the surf
And drags down.

This mouth is shut.
The mouth is clamped cold.
I tell you this tongue is dried.

But the skull, the skull,
The perfect sculpture of bone!—
Around the forehead the fine hair,
Composed to the severest
Lineaments of thought,
Is moulded on peace.

And the strongly wrought features,
That keep in the soul's serenest achievement
The spirit's virtue,
Set the death mask of all mortality,
The impress of that grace.

In the shoal-champed breakers
One wing of the gull
Tilts like a fin through the ribbon of spume
And knifes under.

And all about there the vastness of night
Affirms its sovereignty. There's not a cliff

On the coastline, not a reef
Of the waterways, from the sword-thrust Aleutians
To the scorpion-tailed stinger Cape Horn —
All that staggering declivity
Grasped in the visionary mind and established —
But is sunken under the dark ordainment,
Like a sleeper possessed, like a man
Gone under, like a powerful swimmer
Plunged in a womb-death washed out to sea
And worked back ashore.

The gull's eye,
Skinned to the wave, retains the ocean's
Imponderable compression,
And burns yellow.

The poet is dead. I tell you
The nostrils are narrowed. I say again and again
The strong tongue is broken.

But the owl
Quirks in the cypresses, and you hear
What he says. He is calling for something.
He tucks his head for his mate's
Immemorial whisper. In her answering voice
He tastes the grace-note of his reprieve.
If there is fog in the canyons
The redwoods will know what it means.
The giant sisters
Gather it into their merciful arms
And stroke silence.

When you smell pine resin laced in the salt
You know the dawn wind has veered.

And on the shelf in the gloom,
Blended together, the tall books emerge,
All of a piece. Transparent as membranes
The thin leaves of paper hug their dark thoughts.
They know what he said.

The sea, reaching for life,
Spits up the gull. He falls spread-eagled,
The streaked wings swept on the sand.
When the blind head snaps
The beak krakes at the sky.

Now the night closes.
All the dark's negatory
Decentralization
Quivers toward dawn.

He has gone into death like a stone thrown in the sea.

And in far places the morning
Shrills its episodes of triviality and vice
And one man's passing. Could the ears
That hardly listened in life
Care much less now?

The great tongue
Dries in the mouth. I told you.
The voiceless throat
Cools silence. And the sea-granite eyes.
Washed in the sibilant waters

The stretched lips kiss peace.

The poet is dead.

Nor will ever again hear the sea lions
Grunt in the kelp at Point Lobos.
Nor look to the south when the grunion
Run the Pacific, and the plunging
Shearwaters, insatiable,
Stun themselves in the sea.

List of Works Cited

Alberts, S.S. *A Bibliography of the Works of Robinson Jeffers*. New York, 1933.

Barnet, Sylvan, Morton Berman and William Burto. *A Dictionary of Literary Terms*. Boston, 1960.

Bennett, Joseph. "The Moving Finger Writes," *The Hudson Review*, XVI, iv (Winter 1963-64).

The Bible Designed to Be Read as Living Literature, ed. Ernest Sutherland Bates. New York, 1951.

Campbell, Joseph. *The Hero With a Thousand Faces*. New York, 1949.

Carpenter, Frederic I. *Robinson Jeffers*. New York, 1962.

——————. "Robinson Jeffers and the Torches of Violence," *The Twenties: Poetry and Prose*. Deland, Florida, 1966.

Chesterton, G.K. *The Everlasting Man*. New York, 1925.

Clarke, W. Norris, S.J. "The Limitation of Act by Potency," *The New Scholasticism*, XXVI, ii (April 1952).

D'Arcy, Martin C., S.J. *The Mind and Heart of Love*. 2nd ed., rev., New York, 1956.

Davie, Donald. Review in *The* [Manchester] *Guardian*, XC, xxiv (Thursday, June 17, 1965).

Dodds, E.R. *The Greeks and the Irrational*. Berkeley, 1951.

Eliot, T.S. "The Waste Land," *Collected Poems*. New York, 1936.

Gilbert, Rudolph. *Shine, Perishing Republic*. Boston, 1936.

Graves, Robert. *The White Goddess*. 2nd ed., rev. and enl., New York, 1958.

Gregory, Horace. *The Dying Gladiators and Other Essays*. New York, 1961.

Henderson, Joseph L. and Maud Oakes. *The Wisdom of the Serpent*. New York, 1963.

Hynes, Samuel. Review of *The Utopian Vision of D.H. Lawrence* by Eugene Goodheart, in *Ramparts*, II, iii (Christmas, 1963).

Jung, Carl G. *The Collected Works of C.G. Jung, Vol. 7: Two Essays on Analytical Psychology*, trans. R.F.C. Hull. 2nd ed., New York, 1966.

Kerenyi, C. *Archetypal Images in Greek Religion; Vol. 1: Prometheus*, trans. Ralph Manheim. New York, 1963.

Kitto, H.D.F. *Greek Tragedy*. London, 1939.

Koestler, Arthur. *The Lotus and the Robot*. New York, 1961.

Merton, Thomas. *The Behavior of Titans*. New York, 1961.

Nietzsche, Friedrich. *The Portable Nietzsche*, sel. and trans. Walter Kaufmann. New York, 1954.

Monjian, Mercedes Cunningham. *Robinson Jeffers*. Pittsburgh, 1958.

Mould, D.D.C. Pochin. *Scotland of the Saints*. London, 1952.

Neumann, Erich. *Art and the Creative Unconscious*, trans. Ralph Manheim. New York, 1966.

Ouspensky, P.D. *In Search of the Miraculous*. New York, 1949.

Powell, Lawrence Clark. *Robinson Jeffers*. Pasadena, 1940.

Rexroth, Kenneth. *Assays*. New York, 1961.

Reynolds, Tim. "The Stone-Mason," *Ryoanji*. New York, 1964.

Rosenthal, M.L. *The Modern Poets*. New York, 1960.

Squires, [James] Radcliffe. *The Loyalties of Robinson Jeffers*. Ann Arbor, Michigan, 1956.

Van Doren, Mark. *Mark Van Doren on Great Poems of Western Literature*. New York, 1962.

Van Wyck, William. *Robinson Jeffers*. Los Angeles, 1938.

Werblowsky, R.J.Zwi. *Lucifer and Prometheus*. London, 1952.

Wilder, Amos N. *The Spiritual Aspects of the New Poetry*. 2nd ed., New York, 1940.

Winters, Yvor. *In Defense of Reason*. 3rd ed., Denver, 1947.

Yeats, W.B. "Under Ben Bulben," *The Variorum Edition of the Poems of W.B. Yeats*, ed. Peter Allt and Russell K. Alspach. New York, 1957.

Zimmer, Heinrich. *The King and the Corpse*. New York, 1960.

Index of Names

Abyssinia, 93
Achilles, 92
Aeschylus, 134, 135, 136, 146
Ahab, 121
Agave, 82
Alberts, S. S., 37
Anna Karenina, 30
"Ante Mortem", 34
Anthology of American Poetry, 27
Apocalypse, 50
"Apology for Bad Dreams", 159
Arian, 41
Aristotle, 110, 111, 122
"At the Birth of an Age", 154, 155, 159, 161
"At the Fall of an Age", 92
Auerhahn Press, [163]
Bacchæ, 82
Barclay, The Rev. Dr., 104, 110, 113, 118, 120 ,121, 123, 124, 125, 126, 127, 128, 129, 130, 131, 132, 133, 137, 140, 141, 142, 144, 149, 152, 155, 156, 157, 159, 160, 161, 162
Baudelaire, Charles, 15
Beethoven, Ludwig von, 62
Beginning and the End, The, [57], 62
Bible, 128
"Bird With the Dark Plumes, The" 104
Blackmur, R. P., 29, 31
Blake, William, 36
Buddha, 127, 157
Cain, 135, 137
California, 55

Campbell, Joseph, 30, 126, 127, 132, 139, 142
Carmel, 3, 129, 144, 145, 146
Carpenter, Frederic, 79, 106, 116, 118
Cawdor, 55, 104
Chesterton, Gilbert Keith, 81
Christ, 88, 94, 105, 132, 134, 136, 137, 147, 150, 151, 157, 160
Claire Walker, 55
Clarke, William Norris, S. J., 110
"Coast Road, The" 85
Collingwood, R. V., 113
"Come Little Birds", 159
"Continent's End", 64
Critic, The, [1], 165
d'Annunzio, Gabriele, 86
Dante Alighieri, 3
Davie, Donald, 71, 77
"Dead to Clemenceau, The", 34
"Deer Lay Down Their Bones, The", 165
Dictionary of Literary Terms, A, 39
Dionysos, 96
Dionysos Zagreus, 111
Dodds, E. R., 83, 84
Dostoevski, Fyodor, 107
Egypt, 88
Eliot, Thomas Stearns, 3, 25, 36, 60, [67], 69, 70, 72, 75, 95
Enthusiasm, 123
Erasmus, 134
Ethiopia, 86
Euripides, 82, 122, 124
Evangeline, 109

Excalibur, 42
Faith Heriot, 151, 156
Faust, 110
Fayne Fraser, 55
Fera Martial, 55
"Fifty Years of American Poetry"
  [9]
Flaubert, Gustave, 15
Fletcher, John Gould, 25
Franco, Francisco, 75, 93
Frost, Robert, 3, 16
Gautama, see Buddha
Germany, 93
"Ghosts in England", 42
Gilbert, Rudolph, 106, 107, 110,
  121
Ginsburg, Allen, 25
Goebbels, Joseph, 77
Goethe, Wolfgang, 15, 110, 121
Graves, Robert, 54
Greece, 82, 88
Greek Tragedy, 107
Greeks and the Irrational, The, 83
Greenwich Village, 102
Gregory, Horace, [1], 107
Gudrun, 55, 160
Guernica, 93
Gurdjieff, 139
Hamlet, 110
Helen of Troy, 92
Helen Thurso, 55
"Hellenistics", [67], 80, 85, 86,
  92, 96
Henderson, Joseph L., 125
Hero With a Thousand Faces, The
  126

Hesiod, 134, 135, 136
Hitler, Adolph, 76, 93, 148
Hollywood, 102
Homer, 3
Hood, 55
Hopkins, Gerard Manley, 39, 150
"Humanist's Tragedy, The", 82
"Hurt Hawks", 64
"Hurt Hawks II", 101
Hynes, Samuel, 70, 71, 72, 75, 76,
  77, 79
Ibsen, Henrik, 106
Iliad, The, 109
India, 88
Isaiah, 52
Italy, 93
Jarrell, Randall, [9], 13, 16, 18
Jeffers, Robinson, [1], 3, 4, 6, 7,
  [9], 11, 12, 13, 15, 17, 19, [21],
  23, 25, 26, 27, 29, 30, 31, 32,
  33, 34, 35, 37, 38, 39, 40, 41,
  42, 45, 47, 50, 51, 54, 55, [57],
  59, 60, 61, 63, 64, [67], 69, 70,
  75, 79, 80, 81, 82, 83, 84, 85,
  86, 87, 89, 93, 94, 95, 96, [99],
  101, 104, 105, 107, 108, 109,
  110, 112, 113, 114, 116, 118,
  120, 121, 122, 127, 129, 130,
  131, 132, 136, 137, 138, 139,
  140, 141, 142, 143, 144, 145,
  147, 148, 150, 156, 157, 158,
  159, 161, [163], 165, 166
Jesus, 137, 142, 160
Joyce, James, 3
Judas, 105
Jung, Carl, 125, 132

Kentfield Priory (Kentfield, California), 166
Kerényi, C., 133, 136
King Arthur, 42
King Pentheus, 82
Kitto, H. D. F., 107, 109, 124
Knox, Ronald, 123
Koestler, Arthur, 4
Lao Tze, 157
Lawrence, David Herbert, 25, 26, 36, 37, [67], 70, 71, 72, 75, 76, 79, 80, 81, 95,
Library of Congress, [9], 13
Lindsay, Vachel, 25
Longfellow, 109
Lotus and the Robot, The, 4
Lowell, Robert, 36
Loyalties of Robinson Jeffers, The, 3
Lucifer and Prometheus, 133
Lucretius, 33
Luther, Martin, 41
Manchester Guardian, The, 71
Margrave, 45, 107
Maruca, 120, 156
Mary, 151
Mayakovsky, Vladimir, 78, 85
Medea, 124
Merton, Thomas, 134, 135
Milton, John, 3, 110, 131
Modern Poets, The, 23
Mohammed, 88
Monjian, Mercedes Cunningham 107
Monterey, 153
Moses, 88

Mould, D.D.C. Pochin, 26
Mount Cithæron, 83
Mount Sinai, 127, 137
Mussolini, Benito, 75, 86
Myrtle Cartwright, 154
McPherson, Aimee Semple, 146
Natalia Morhead, 156
National Poetry Festival, 1962 [9], 13
Neumann, Erich, 143
New Directions, 6
Nietzsche, Friedrich, 15, 16, 76, 117
"Night", 64
Oedipus, 5
Old Vasquez, 150
"On an Anthology of Chinese Poems", 61
Onorio Vasquez, 144, 145, 148, 150, 151, 154
Ossian, 26, 27, 28, 33
"Ossian's Grave", 27
Oppenheim, James, 25
Orpheus, 97
Ouspensky, P. D., 139
"Passenger Pigeons", [57]
"Pelicans", [9]
Pico Blanco, 137
Plato, 111
Plotinus, 111
Plumed Serpet, The, 77
"Poet Without Critics", [1]
Poetry, 7
Point Pinos, 151
Point Sur, 146, 150, 151, 155, 156
Point Sur, see *Women at Point Sur, The*

"Post Mortem", [21], 27, 69, 101, 165

Pound, Ezra, 3, 23, 24, 25, 28, 29, 36, 37, [67], 69, 70, 71, 72, 74, 75, 95

Powell, Lawrence Clark, 105, 127, [163]

Prairie Schooner, The, [9]

Prometheus, 132, 133, 134, 135, 136

Prometheus Bound, 108

Randal Morhead, 156

Ramparts, [57], 70

Raskolnikov, 107

"Rearmament", 82, 92

Rexroth, Kenneth, 7, 114

Reynolds, Tim, [1], 7, 8

Rimbaud, Arthur, 15

Roan Stallion, 19, 102, 103, 107, 112, 118

Roan Stallion, Tamar and Other Poems, 102, 103

Rodman, Selden, 78

Rome, 6, 111

Rosenthal, M.L., 23, 29

Russia, 93

Saint Patrick, 26

San Francisco Chronicle, The, 166

San Francisco Museum of Art, 165

San Francisco Poetry Festival, 1962, [163], 165, 166

Sandburg, Carl, 25

Satan, 110, 131

Schevill, James, 165

Scotland of the Saints, 26

"Seafarer", 24, 28, 29

Selected Poetry of Robinson Jeffers, The, 11, 105

Shakespeare, William, 106, 109

"Shine, Empire", 79, 80

"Shine, Perishing Republic", 79, 80

"Shine, Republic", 79

Siegel, Eli, 25

Southern California, 146

Spain, 93

Squires, [James] Radcliffe, 3, 5, 29, 69, 106, 112, 115, 122

Stevens, Wallace, 16

"Stone-Mason, The", 8

Tamar, 19, 102, 109, 130, 159, 160, 161

Tamar Cauldwell, 54, 132, 133, 159, 160

"Theory of Truth", 157

"To Death", 165

Tolstoy, Leo, 14, 29, 30

Tor House, 3

"Tower Beyond Tragedy, The", 146, 161

"Trap, The", [67]

"Triad", [21]

"Tribute to Robinson Jeffers, A", [1]

Una Jeffers, 37

"Under Ben Bulben", 77, 96

Untermeyer, Louis, 27

Van Doren, Mark, 109

Van Wyck, William, 88

Versailles, 86

Wagner, Richard, 76, 148

Waste Land, The, 35

Werblowsky, R.J. Zwi, 133
Whitman, Walt, 24, 25, 26, 36, 37, 38, 88
Wilder, Amos, 116
"Windhover", 150
Winters, Yvor, 101, 114, 115, 116, 117, 120
Wisdom of the Serpent, The, 125
Women at Point Sur, The, 19, 101, 102, 105, 106, 109, 112, 114, 116, 117, 120, 122, 123, 124, 127, 129, 131, 137, 140, 141, 156, 157, 160, 161

"Woodrow Wilson", 34, 45
Woolf, Virginia, 11
World War I, 25, 74, 137, 149
World War II, 122
Xenophon, 88
Yale Collection of American Literature, 144, 150
Yeats, William Butler, 3, [67], 69, 70, 71, 72, 75, 78, 87, 95, 137
Zaturenska, Marya, 107
Zeus, 135
Zimmer, Heinrich, 117, 148